MODERN
NATIONS
—OF THE—
WORLD

SCOTLAND

SCOTLAND

BY WILLIAM W. LACE

LUCENT BOOKS
P.O. BOX 289011
SAN DIEGO, CA 92198-9011

On Cover: Princes St., Edinburgh, Scotland

Library of Congress Cataloging-in-Publication Data

Lace, William W.
  Scotland / by William W. Lace
      p.   cm. — (Modern nations of the world)
Includes bibliographical references and index.
Summary: Discusses Scotland, its land, people, monarchy, history, politics,
present-day issues, and popular culture.
  ISBN 1-56006-703-9 (hardcover : alk. paper)
  1. Scotland—Juvenile literature. [1. Scotland.] I. Title. II. Series.
   DA762 .L235 2001
   941.1—dc21   00-008757

Copyright © 2001 by Lucent Books, Inc.
P.O. Box 289011, San Diego, CA 92198-9011
Printed in the U.S.A.

CONTENTS

INTRODUCTION
A LAND APART

Scotland shares much with England, its larger neighbor. The people speak the same language, are ruled by the same queen, fly the same flag. At first, it is hard to tell, driving across the border, that one has entered another country. Hills, farms, and villages appear the same; only the highway number seems to have changed. And yet Scotland is, indeed, a land apart—a country with its own proud heritage and fiercely independent spirit.

The further north one travels, the greater the differences become. Signs point the way to places with names such as Lochmaben, Innerleithen, and Kirkmuirhill. Shopkeepers have the distinctive Scots burr in their speech; the banknotes they hand out bear the likeness of King Robert the Bruce, whose victory over the English in 1314 regained Scotland its former independence—temporarily.

The low rolling hills give way to heather-crowned mountains looming high over secluded valleys and deep mysterious lochs (lakes). A lone piper in full Highland dress may well be standing by the roadside where tourists stop for the breathtaking views, the wail of his instrument echoing through the glens. It is a scene unmistakably Scottish and definitely not English.

A LIVING HERITAGE

Bagpipes, kilts, heather, lochs—they are not only the stuff of Scottish legends and of tourist attractions but also part of everyday life. A businessman walking along the streets of Inverness in a kilt draws no more attention than someone wearing cowboy boots in Dallas. Pipe bands are to Scottish schools what marching bands are to their American counterparts.

The distinctiveness of Scotland stems first from its geography. Modern travel has brought London and Edinburgh only a few hours apart, but for most of its history Scotland was so distant and land travel so difficult that even Ireland and France (although separated by water) were more accessible. Thus the Scots felt the influence of England less keenly than other peoples of the British Isles—especially in the Scottish Highlands where rugged terrain cut the clans, or family groups, off from one another, let alone from England.

Scotland's geographical isolation was also a prime factor in its cultural isolation. When the Romans conquered Britain in the first century A.D., they encountered fierce resistance from the tribes then inhabiting Scotland. The conflict was so fierce that the Romans eventually decided to seal off the area rather than expend the effort necessary to conquer it. Under the emperor Hadrian, a seventy-three-mile wall was constructed to protect Roman Britain. Behind that wall Scotland developed differently than did England, with more influence coming from Scandinavia and Ireland than from Europe.

A piper in traditional Scottish dress plays his bagpipes with the rugged hills of the Highlands in the background.

Royal procession in the city of Edinburgh prior to the ceremony of the official opening of the Scottish Parliament, July 1, 1999.

ENDURING DIFFERENCES

Part of the reason why the cultural differences between Scotland and England have persisted is that the Scots have wanted it that way. For centuries England was the enemy and sometimes the overlord. Attempts by the English to strip away Scotland's heritage and freedom made the Scots all the more determined to retain and to celebrate that heritage. They have accepted—many of them grudgingly—being part of a United Kingdom *with* England, but resist mightily the notion of being thought a part *of* England.

As the twentieth century ended, the independent spirit of Scotland found new expression. On July 1, 1999, Queen Elizabeth II opened the first Scottish Parliament in almost three hundred years. Even though the Scots were uncertain about the exact function of the new body and were (with characteristic thrift) concerned about its cost, they nevertheless enthusiastically welcomed the opportunity to express their identity as a nation apart.

THE LAND

Scotland's geography is most often thought of in terms of the Highlands, with their scenic mountains and glens. The country actually contains a variety of landscapes and natural resources, all of which have shaped the plant and the animal life and the way in which the Scots live and work.

Scotland is located at the northern end of the island of Britain. It is bordered on the south by England, on the east by the North Sea, and on the north and west by the Atlantic Ocean. It covers 30,421 square miles, but the area is not a solid mass of land and includes almost eight hundred islands. These range from tiny offshore lumps of rock to the Isle of Skye, which is slightly smaller than Rhode Island.

Steep cliffs rise sharply behind the village and harbor of Gardenstown in Banffshire in northeast Scotland.　9

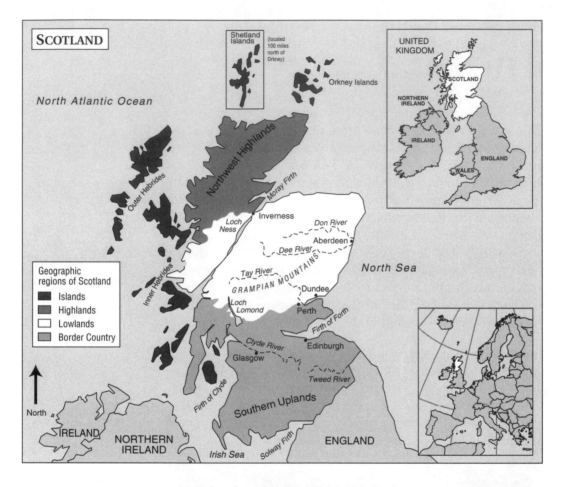

Scotland and England have long been uneasy neighbors, not only through human conflict during much of their recorded history, but also from geologic cataclysms millions of years ago. The two countries originally were part of different land masses separated by the thousand-mile-wide Iapetus Sea. As the continents took shape, these land masses were crushed together and the sea disappeared. The colliding land masses made the earth's crust buckle forming the hills and mountains of Scotland, most ranges running from northeast to southwest.

The collision also created deep cracks, or "faults," in the land. There are two major fault lines in Scotland, and they divide the country into three distinct geographical regions. One fault line runs southwest from the city of Aberdeen on the east coast to the firth, or estuary, of the River Clyde, west of the city of Glasgow. The second also runs southwest, from Dunbar south of the mouth of the River Forth to Girvan on the channel between the Atlantic Ocean and the Irish Sea.

THE HIGHLANDS

North of the first line, encompassing two-thirds of the land area of Scotland, are the Highlands and the western and northern island groups. The Highlands were shaped by successive waves of glaciers, rivers of ice that scooped out long deep valleys known as glens, as they moved slowly southward over thousands of years. The last of the glaciers melted about ten thousand years ago, the water filling the numerous lochs, some of them hundreds of feet deep.

The largest of these glens, Glen More, stands out on a map like a great gash running southwest from the city of Inverness. Much of its length is taken up by one of the most outstanding natural features in Scotland—Loch Ness, which is twenty-three miles long, more than seven hundred feet deep, and supposedly inhabited by a prehistoric monster.

Glen More divides the Highlands into two zones. To the north lie the Northwest Highlands, the least inhabited region in mainland Britain. The area, although of spectacular natural

Eilean Donan castle on Loch Duich, Highlands.

Located on the Clyde River, Glasgow has become a major industrial center.

beauty, is almost totally unfit for farming because of the steep hills and rocky soil. Only along the coast and in the islands do some small farms known as crofts exist. Even sheep find grazing difficult in the Northwest Highlands because of the lack of vegetation.

South of Glen More are the equally inhospitable Grampian Mountains, at the western edge of which is Ben Nevis, at 4,406 feet the tallest peak in Britain. The southern and eastern parts of the Grampian region, however, are gentler and support extensive sheep raising in the south and some of the world's finest beef cattle in the east.

South of the Highlands, between the two fault lines, are the Central Lowlands, much smaller in size but vastly more importantly economically and politically. The estuaries of three major rivers—the Forth and the Tay in the east and the Clyde in the west—cut into the area and each estuary boasts a major city: Edinburgh, Dundee, and Glasgow, respectively. Because they are located so far inland, these ports have a distinct advantage over those on the coast since goods can be transported further inland more quickly.

A WEALTH OF RESOURCES

The Central Lowlands have an additional advantage: They contain most of Scotland's coal and iron deposits, remnants of the time millions of years ago when the area that became Scotland was located on the equator and much of the land was a tropical rain forest. This wealth of natural resources, combined with the excellent port facilities and the history of the region as the political capital of Scotland, led during the Industrial Revolution of the 1800s to the advent of a modern manufacturing society—especially in the Glasgow area—and a rapid rise in population. As a result, more than three-fourths of the population of Scotland live roughly within ten miles on either side of a line from Edinburgh to Glasgow.

Just as the Highlands are not truly high as compared with the earth's other mountainous regions, so the Lowlands are not truly low in the same sense as are the coastal plains of the United States. The valleys of the Forth and Clyde Rivers are dotted with hills, many of them extinct volcanoes. Edinburgh Castle sits on a volcanic plug 250 feet above the valley floor, while the nearby peak known as Arthur's Seat is 820 feet high.

In addition to being rich in mineral resources, the Central Lowlands have some of the best farming soil in Scotland. The Strathmore and Fife areas just north of the Firth of Forth have a rich, sandstone-based topsoil ideal for wheat, barley, and oats. Here, too, is the chief potato-growing part of the country. Oats and beans predominate in the Lothian area south and west of Edinburgh, with sheep farming in the higher elevations. Further west the Clyde valley supports pig and poultry farming as well as grains and fruits such as strawberries, currants, and plums.

South of the Central Lowlands, below the Dunbar-Girvan fault line, are the Southern Uplands. The name derives from the series of hills that run from east to west across the center of the region as well as from the Cheviot Hills on the southern edge that form the border with England. Unlike

Central Lowlands farm on Loch Tay, Perthshire.

the Highland mountains, which are composed of some of the hardest rocks on earth, such as granite, the hills of the Southern Uplands are mostly shale and slate. Wind and rain have eroded these softer materials, making the hills lower, seldom more than two thousand feet high, and more rounded than their northern counterparts.

A LIVESTOCK AREA

Livestock raising dominates agriculture in the western part of the Southern Uplands region (Ayrshire and Galloway), with sheep at the higher elevations and cattle, mostly dairy cattle, in the valleys and on the coast. Some barley and oats are raised, but most of the crops are roots and grasses used as fodder for the livestock.

The best sheep-farming land in Scotland is found to the east on the hilltops of the Tweed River basin. The Tweed valley itself, known as the Merse, is one of the most fertile areas in the country, with highly mechanized farms growing grasses, oats, wheat, barley, turnips, and sugar beets for market as well as for fodder.

Although the eastern part of the Southern Uplands is now one of the most prosperous areas of Scotland, life was very difficult for its inhabitants in past centuries. Known as the

Cattle farming in the Southern Uplands, near Bermersyde.

Border Country, it is the narrowest part of Britain—only about thirty miles across—and was long the route taken by English invaders. Ruined castles and abbeys are mute reminders of the incessant warfare that ravaged the region.

The geography of Scotland changes just as dramatically from west to east as it does from north to south, especially in the Highlands. Most of the country's 787 islands lie off the western coast, where upthrusts of hard stone were separated from the mainland by the movement and melting of the glaciers. The land has been further eroded by the pounding of the Atlantic surf and the gales that whip down from Greenland. As a result most of the west coast is rocky and inhospitable, with travel difficult and settlements few and far between.

The east coast has had a gentler history. Washed by the much calmer North Sea and composed of softer soils, the region has developed land suitable for farming and livestock. The coastal areas contain long sloping sandy beaches, on some of which have been built the most famous golf courses in the world, including Saint Andrew's and Carnoustie.

VARIABLE CLIMATE

Just as variable as Scotland's geography—and contributing a great deal to it—is the climate. Scotland has a reputation for being cold, wet, and windy. For the most part that reputation is deserved. Yet the weather is not as bad as one might think given the fact that Edinburgh is on a more northerly latitude than Moscow and that the northernmost point on the mainland is less than six hundred miles south of the Arctic Circle.

Scotland's weather is mitigated by the Gulf Stream, a current of warm water and accompanying warm air that flows from the Gulf of Mexico to the British Isles. As a result, the temperature in Edinburgh in Januay is thirty-seven degrees Fahrenheit—hardly balmy, but far warmer than Moscow's average of nine degrees below zero.

The downside of the Gulf Stream is that the warmer moist air frequently clashes with cold dry air moving southeast from Greenland. The resulting interplay of air currents renders Scottish weather extremely unpredictable. It is not at all unusual to have two or three alternating periods of rain and sunshine on the same day. Rainfall is more frequent and heavier in the west, where large areas receive more than

THE LOCH NESS MONSTER

In the late sixth century, Saint Columba journeyed to the northern city of Inverness to attempt to convert the king of the Picts to Christianity. On the way, according to legend, he was attacked by a fearsome monster as he passed by Loch Ness. Drawing strength from his faith, he defeated the monster and proceeded to Inverness, where he was successful in winning over the Pictish king. Ever since, stories have persisted that some sort of monster, called an *each uisge*, or "water horse" in Gaelic, inhabits the seven-hundred-foot depths of Loch Ness.

There have been numerous sightings—or reported sightings—of the Loch Ness Monster throughout the centuries. Photographs purported to be that of the monster appeared in the 1930s. One of the most famous showed what might be a long, slender neck emerging from the water.

In 1933 two English tourists claimed the monster crossed the highway in front of their car. As quoted in *The Land and People of Scotland* by James Meek, one of the tourists said, "It was a loathsome sight. It seems futile to describe it because it was like nothing I had ever read about or seen. It was terrible. Its colour, so far as the body was concerned, could be called a dark elephant gray. It looked like a huge snail with a long neck."

But despite round-the-clock watches, underwater cameras, and submarines equipped with sonar, there has been no confirmation of the monster's existence. This hasn't stopped "Nessie" from becoming the subject of many a souvenir, with the monster's likeness on everything from topiary to T-shirts to plush toys.

eighty inches per year and annual rainfall of nearly two hundred inches has been recorded in some spots.

Rainfall is less in the east but still averages more than forty inches per year in most places. The east, however, does not feel the full effect of the Gulf Stream and thus is colder. Although blizzards are rare, most of the east will experience snow more than twenty days per year as compared with fewer than ten days per year on the west coast.

EFFECTS OF WIND

Another factor that affects Scottish weather is the wind, which whips in from the Atlantic and swirls through the mountains and glens. The strong wind causes weather patterns to move swiftly from west to east most of the year. The winds are gale force, up to 126 miles per hour, on the west coast and especially in the Orkney and Shetland island groups to the north. Winters are especially fierce in the Shetlands, with gales much of the time, subfreezing temperatures, and only a few hours of dim daylight.

The winds have had a dramatic effect on the Scottish landscape. Most of the mountains of the Highlands are bare of trees; it is simply too windy for them to take root and grow in the soil. Even without trees, however, the mountains have a wild beauty, especially in the fall when purple heather adorns the ridges.

Groves of birch, beech, ash, and alder trees are found at the lower elevations and in sheltered areas of the mountains, but the oaks which once covered most of Scotland have largely disappeared, cut down long ago for constructing buildings and ships. Today, only about 15 percent of Scotland is forested, and more than 90 percent of that area consists of commercial plantations of conifers such as spruce, pine, larch, and fir. While forestry has become increasingly important economically,

The ruins of a structure stand alone on the bare, windswept landscape of the Shetland Islands.

MUNROS

In most countries mountains are just "mountains." In Scotland, they are called "Munros" after Sir Hugh Thomas Munro, a nineteenth-century climbing enthusiast. Shortly after he founded the Scottish Mountaineering Club in 1889, Munro set out to survey and catalog every peak three thousand feet or higher. He published his list in 1891, and the mountains on it quickly became known as Munros.

Ever since, the mark of success among Scottish mountaineers is to become a "Munroist," one who has successfully scaled all 277 Munros. Reverend Aeneas Robertson was the first to do so, completing the list by climbing Meall Dearg in 1901. Many have accomplished the feat since, but Munro himself was not among them, failing in several attempts to climb Sgurr Alasdair on the Isle of Skye.

many Scots object to the way the trees have been planted in neat, regimented rows, contrasting with the surrounding natural beauty.

The mountains, woodlands, and wetland meadows of Scotland contain distinct types of wildflowers and shrubs. Heather and tough grasses cover many mountainsides along with mosses and worts, but there are plenty of Arctic-Alpine plants such as gentians, forget-me-nots, trailing azaleas, foxtail, cat's-tail, and saxifrage. Wildflowers and ferns also thrive in the natural forests, though not in commercial forests because of the thick blanket of needles. The most common species are bluebells and primroses, the latter one of Scotland's traditional symbols.

THE THISTLE

An even stronger symbol of Scotland is the thistle with its prickly leaves and beautiful purple flower, which it is said, reflect both the toughness and grandeur of the Scots. Thistles once thrived in lowland meadows, along with cornflowers, wild poppies, and marigolds, but all are rapidly vanishing as more wetland meadows are drained and used for farming.

The increase of farming and urbanization has also curtailed wildlife in lowland areas, but many species thrive in the northern woodlands where humans have made few imprints. Eagles, hawks, falcons, osprey, and kestrels soar above the mountains and coastal cliffs, seeking prey below. Trees furnish nests for owls, woodpeckers, and crossbills.

Many kinds of grouse inhabit Scotland and are much prized by hunters. The largest and most unusual is the capercaille, from the Gaelic words for "horse of the woods." Once extinct in Scotland, it was reintroduced from Sweden and is so large, weighing up to twelve pounds, that it is often mistaken for a turkey at first sight. The capercaille is as aggressive as it is large and has even been known to attack humans when its territory is threatened.

Further up highland slopes are the red grouse, Scotland's most popular game bird. At even higher elevations is the ptarmigan, an arctic bird whose plumage in winter is white so that it can blend in with snow.

The west coast and islands are havens for hundreds of varieties of sea birds. More than half the world's population of gannets breed in Scotland, and an estimated fifty-five thousand pairs of puffins—appealing little birds with plump bodies and multicolored beaks—dwell in the Orkney Islands. The country is also the winter home of huge flocks of arctic geese that migrate from Greenland each autumn.

THE PREDATORS

In addition to human hunters, the birds of Scotland have several natural enemies, primarily the fox and the wildcat. Foxes, mostly the red fox, are found in every part of the country. Even in the center of Edinburgh, roadside signs warn motorists to be wary of these fearless predators. The Scottish wildcat, found mostly in the Highlands, is one of the few varieties left in Europe.

A Scottish wildcat crouches in a tree with its prey. The Scottish wildcat is one of the few wildcats left in Europe.

The Highland cow's thick fur allows it to thrive in the cold climate of the Highlands.

It is not large, hardly bigger than a housecat, but can be recognized by its short ringed bushy tail.

The woodlands of Scotland are inhabited by many of the same species found throughout Britain and most of Europe—stoats, weasels, and badgers. Badgers are found mostly in the Southern Uplands, but, like foxes, have even made themselves at home in the parklands of large cities. Scotland also is the home to an estimated ten thousand otters, the last remaining in Britain.

Another archenemy of the bird population is the mink. They were originally imported from North America for commercial purposes, but most of the mink farms failed to make money and were closed. Many of the inhabitants, however, escaped to the wild where they have become well established.

Larger animals include wild sheep and goats that—like the mink—have made their escape over the centuries from farmyards. The largest mammal in Scotland, however, is the red deer that roam in large herds over the Highlands. Called the "Monarchs of the Forest" and once almost hunted into extinction, these majestic animals have made a comeback, rising in number from fifteen thousand in the 1950s to more than three hundred thousand in the mid-1990s. Indeed, they have grown so numerous and spread to so many farming areas that the number allowed to be shot by hunters each year has risen dramatically.

Some of the most famous animals in Scotland are domesticated. The Highland cattle with their long horns and shaggy red coats are a common sight. Especially adapted to the cold weather, they have been bred since the fifteen hundreds. Far to the north are two species for which the Shetland Islands are famous, the tough wiry Shetland ponies and the fluffy Shetland sheepdogs, smaller versions of the collie.

FISHING AND THE DISCOVERY OF OIL

Scotland is surrounded on three sides by the sea and is crisscrossed by hundreds of rivers and lochs. It is little wonder, then, that fish and other marine animals have played a large part in the Scottish economy. Anglers come from all over the world to try their luck in the fast-flowing rivers and streams. Popular catches include trout, pike, perch, and lamprey, but the king of the rivers is the salmon. A longtime target of both humans and animals, the wild salmon is in danger of disappearing. The population has been lowered dramatically by overfishing, an

JOHN MUIR

The loveliness of the Scottish landscape has had a profound effect on many people, but on no one more so than John Muir. Muir, in turn, has had a profound effect on the environmental movement and the preservation of wilderness areas.

Born in Dunbar, Scotland, in 1838, Muir developed his love of nature from the many hours exploring the beaches of East Lothian and the Lammermuir Hills. He emigrated with his family to the United States when he was eleven, but retained a fondness for his native land, as quoted in *The Nature of Scotland*, edited by Magnus Magnusson and Graham White:

> When I was a boy in Scotland I was fond of everything that was wild, and all my life I've been growing fonder and fonder of wild places and wild creatures. Fortunately, around my native town of Dunbar, by the stormy North Sea, there was no lack of wilderness . . . with red-blooded playmates, wild as myself, I loved to wander in the fields to hear the birds sing, and along the seashore to gaze and wonder at the shells and seaweeds, eels and crabs, in the pools among the rocks when the tide was low.

Muir founded the Sierra Club in 1882 and was instrumental in having Yosemite declared a national park in 1905. In Scotland, the organization dedicated to conserving and protecting the wilderness was named the John Muir Trust in 1983.

Scottish-born naturalist, explorer, and writer John Muir.

Fishing boats in Pittenweam harbor near Fife. Fishing is an important industry in Scotland.

increase in the salmon-eating seal population of the western islands, and disease cause by sea lice that breed in fish farms and spread to streams. The wild salmon swim up these streams to spawn.

Out to sea, fishing continues to be a mainstay of Scottish industry. Lobsters, crabs, prawns, and shrimp are plentiful. Herring, once the primary commercial catch, was overfished after World War II and now is less important than mackerel and cod. Other commercial fish include whiting, halibut, and skate.

One of the most important factors of Scottish geography is found not on the land or in the sea, but under the sea. In 1969 large deposits of oil were discovered offshore in the North Sea. Although most of the wells are in Scottish waters, the revenue goes to the British government—a sore point among the Scots. The oil industry, however, has furnished thousands of jobs and made the city of Aberdeen one of the petroleum capitals of the world.

Scotland is a lovely land, but lovely in a wild, sometimes forbidding way. Much of the landscape is harsh; much of the weather is harsh. Until the discovery of oil in the North Sea, Scotland was never rich in natural resources. It has never been an easy or gentle place in which to live, but the very toughness of the land has bred a similar toughness and determination in its people.

THE PEOPLE

Ethnic stereotypes are sometimes the product of historical facts. If the Scots are thrifty to the point of stinginess, as reputed, it is because they have had to be frugal after centuries of eking out a living in an often harsh and poor land. If they are stubborn, it is because they have had to be unyielding in order to preserve their heritage from being swallowed up and lost. If they are proud, it is because they have much to be proud of, a tradition of courage and defiance that has enabled them to maintain at least a degree of independence.

If the Scots are intelligent, quick-witted, and resourceful—as witnessed by the many outstanding engineers, inventors, and scientists they have produced—it is because universal education has been the rule for more than two hundred years, long before it came to most of Europe. If they are hard-working and industrious, it is because of a centuries'-old tradition of strict Presbyterianism emphasizing the virtue of labor.

The Scots have long had the reputation of being dour and unemotional. To the extent that this is true, the characteristic

Three residents of Jura, one of the Inner Hebrides islands off Scotland's west coast. 23

Scots' reserve also stems from their religious tradition. The Kirk, as the Scots refer to their church hierarchy, frowned on public demonstrations of affection or emotion. At times, however, the Scots' feelings pour forth, as if they have been bottled up too long. The exuberant celebrations at New Year's are one example, and there are no soccer fans more thunderously enthusiastic.

A REALISTIC OUTLOOK

Likewise, the legacy of poverty has played a role in the Scots' outlook. The Scottish viewpoint is that life has never been easy, is not supposed to be easy, and should not be expected to be easy. As a result, there is an air of pessimism as if every silver lining must have a cloud.

This is not to say the Scots are unfriendly. On the contrary, they are warm and genuine toward one another and in their welcome of visitors. They have a lively sense of humor, even if it tends sometimes to be wry and aimed at themselves.

The Scots love their country and are fiercely protective of their traditions. They may make fun of themselves and their customs, but that does not mean they will tolerate such comments from an outsider. Quick to point out Scotland's shortcomings, they are equally quick to defend it. Their often gruff exterior belies an interior depth of patriotism. The Scots may be just as sentimental about their country as the Irish; they just don't show it as openly.

Edinburgh Castle and Arthur's Seat rise above the Scottish capital of Edinburgh.

But, although the Scots have usually presented a united picture to the rest of the world, they have a history of disunity—Highlander against Lowlander, Protestant against Catholic, clan against clan. Author Robert Louis Stevenson, an Edinburgh native, wrote, "Scotland is indefinable: It has no unity except on the map. Two languages, many dialects, innumerable forms of piety, and countless local patriotisms and prejudices, part us from ourselves."[1]

As the twentieth century drew to an end, Scotland's chief division was between urban and rural Scots. Scotland is overwhelmingly rural with only about 170 people per square mile as compared to more than 900 in En-

SCOTLAND'S THREE LANGUAGES

Three languages—Gaelic, Scots, and English—
are traditional to Scotland. English has become so dominant,
however, that the other two are in danger of disappearing.

Gaelic was for centuries the chief language of the country
and the only language spoken by most of its people, especially
those in the Highlands and in the western areas. As the use of
English spread, particularly in the 1700s, Gaelic began to be
heard less and less. At the end of the twentieth century only
about sixty thousand native Gaelic speakers remained, most
of them in the outer Hebrides Islands. Although the language
has had somewhat of a revival thanks to government-funded
broadcasts, it survives mostly in geographical place names
such as *ben* (mountain), *loch* (lake), and *eilean* (island).

Experts argue whether Scots is a dialect of English or, as the
Scots much prefer to think, a separate language altogether.
Like modern English, it developed from a combination of Anglo-Saxon (Old English) and Norman French and many of the
words are similar, such as *coo* (cow), *auld* (old), and *kirk*
(church). Scots also contains some of the words most associated with Scotland, such as *lassie*, *wee*, and *bairn* (baby). Scots
contractions are different from those in English, like *dinnae*
(didn't), *cannae* (can't), and *willnae* (won't).

No such thing as "pure" Scots exists. It varies widely according to region, and what many visitors assume is Scots actually
is a mixture of Scots and English. The language survives
mostly as the chief ingredient in the English heard throughout
Scotland, with its colorful phrases and distinct accent.

gland. Even that figure is deceiving. More than three out of every
four of Scotland's estimated 5.1 million people live in the Central Lowlands, in and around the cities of Glasgow, Edinburgh,
and Dundee; however, the Highlands, encompassing two-
thirds of the land area, or an area slightly smaller than West Vir-
ginia, has a population of only about 300,000. As a result, the
Lowlanders tend to look on their Highland countrymen as
rough and uncouth, while the Highlanders resent their neighbors' comparative wealth and accuse them of being more English than Scottish.

URBAN RIVALRY

Rivalry also exists among the cities, primarily between Edinburgh and Glasgow. Glasgow, with a metropolitan population

NAMING SCOTLAND

The heritage of the different peoples who combined to make up Scotland is found not only among their descendants, but also in the names of cities, towns, and villages. Many give clues as to whether the people who first settled there were Pictish, Celtic, Norse, or Anglo-Saxon.

The southern part of the Highlands abounds with Pictish names. The Pictish word for farm was *pit*, which gave rise to the towns of Pitlorchy, Pitsligo, and Pittenweem. The place where a river flowed into the sea or a lake was an *aber*, hence Aberdeen, Abernethy, Aberfeldy.

On the other hand, the Gaelic word for an *aber* was *inver*, giving us Inverness, Inverary, and many others. Likewise, one can be certain that Glengarry, Glencoe, and Glenfiddich are in valleys. The word *kin* meant a head or top, leading to Kencardine, Kinross, and Kinloss.

The early Angles gave English-sounding names such as Haddinton, Coldingham, and Crookham. Also of English origin are the many *burghs*, or market towns, of which Edinburgh is the best known.

Norse names are found mostly in the Western Isles, the Orkneys and Shetlands, and in the far north of the mainland. There's nothing particularly fair about Fair Isle in the Shetlands, but the name doesn't refer to the weather, instead coming from *faar*, the old Norse word for sheep. And some might think it odd that one of the northernmost points on the mainland is Sutherland (southland) until one remembers that Sutherland was considerably south of most of the Norse strongholds.

---

of about 1.4 million is the fourth-largest city in Great Britain and the industrial heart of Scotland. With labor it has largely overcome a reputation (once well-deserved) as a sooty, grimy manufacturing city blighted by urban decay. It boasts some of the country's finest museums and some of the most striking modern architecture in Europe. Indeed, it is as if Glasgow, unable to match the medieval charm of old Edinburgh, has set out to make its mark in a distinctly different way.

Edinburgh, on the other hand, has the advantage of centuries of tradition and history. Inhabited for more than two thousand years and Scotland's capital for the last five hundred, it has a rich heritage unmatched by any other city in Great Britain except for London. Edinburghers are justifiably proud of their scenic main street—the Royal Mile—with Edinburgh

Castle at one end and Holyrood Palace at the other. It is only fit-
ting, they insist much to the Glaswegians' displeasure, that
Scotland's new Parliament building is under construction here.

CULTURAL DIFERENCES

In addition to urban-rural and urban-urban divisions, Scotland
also is divided culturally by language and religion. Although English is universally spoken, Gaelic—derived from the language of
the early Celts and invaders from Ireland—still is heard in the
Glasgow area, in the Northwest Highlands, and in the Western
Isles. Even though fewer than 5 percent of Scots speak Gaelic,
they hold fast to the traditional tongue, insisting that signs on
highways and in other public places be in both languages.

RELIGIOUS DIFFERENCES

The Gaelic-speaking part of Scotland is also the region where
the Roman Catholic religion is strongest. Most Scottish
Catholics are descendants of immigrants from Ireland in the
nineteenth century. They attend different schools than their
Protestant neighbors and are strongly sympathetic to the
Catholics of Northern Ireland in their struggles with Britain.
While there is little violence between Catholic and Protestant,
as in Northern Ireland, there nevertheless is a degree of dis-
comfort. Intermarriage is infrequent, and the division extends
even to sports, where Catholics and Protestants cheer for
"their" soccer teams.

PRODUCTS OF THE PAST

Who are these people known as the Scots? Where did they
come from? The unity and divisions of Scotland are products
of thousands of years of settlement and invasion. The Scots
are not a single people but a combination of peoples who
merged and mingled, fought and feuded, and eventually
forged themselves into a nation.

The first people to reach Scotland arrived about 7000
B.C. during the Mesolithic, or Middle Stone Age. They may
have crossed an ancient land bridge from the European
mainland, but some experts think they may have used
crude boats of leather stretched across wooden frames.
Lacking the tools or the knowledge to form agricultural
communities, they clung to the coastline, hunting game
and gathering shellfish.

The ruins of ancient stone dwellings on the Orkney Islands. Beginning in about 4500 B.C., Neolithic peoples built stone monuments and dome-shaped huts in Scotland.

The Mesolithic people were followed around 4500 B.C. by those of the Neolithic, or New Stone Age. A more settled farming people, they not only cultivated grain and began keeping cattle and sheep, but they also erected stone monuments and dome-shaped dwellings, many of which are still to be seen in the Orkney and Shetland Islands. The Neolithic Age gave way about 1800 B.C. to the Bronze Age, when people across Britain began to work metal and greatly improve both weapons and farming implements. They have been termed by archaeologists the "Beaker Folk" from the shape of their drinking vessels.

THE CELTS

The old societies were brushed aside starting about 300 B.C. with the arrival of the Celts in Scotland and the dawn of the Iron Age. Originating in Central Europe around Austria, these warlike people, with their iron weapons and chariots, swept across Western Europe and into Britain. They built massive hilltop forts and squat stone towers known as *brochs*, hundreds of which still survive in north Scotland.

Collectively, the various Celtic tribes who crossed the English Channel are known as the Britons. They fought one another for centuries until, in the first century A.D., a common enemy appeared—the Romans. The Romans began their prolonged invasions of Britain in A.D. 54 and in A.D. 81 moved north against what became modern-day Scotland, which they called Caledonia. The governor, Agricola, established a base at Stirling on the upper reaches of the River Forth, then marched northward and defeated the Caledonians at Mons Graupius, probably somewhere in the Grampian Mountain region.

Had Agricola been allowed to consolidate his victory, the history of Scotland might have been far different. But in 84 he was ordered to withdraw. Agricola's nephew, the historian Tacitus, grumbled, "Britain conquered then at once thrown away."[2]

Rome had decided that Scotland was not worth the trouble of conquering. The posture became purely defensive. In 121 the emperor Hadrian visited Britain and ordered the building of a wall to keep the barbarian tribes away from the more settled south. Hadrian's Wall stretched seventy-three miles from near the present city of Newcastle upon Tyne in England west to the Solway Firth. Twenty feet high and with forts every mile or so, it was an impressive feat of architecture; long segments of it survive. Later a second wall, the Antonine, was built to the north from the Forth to the Clyde, but it was abandoned sixty years later.

HADRIAN'S WALL

Hadrian's Wall kept Scotland and what would later become England apart, and this physical separation had major implications. Roman civilization, which had a lasting impact on England, never took hold in Scotland. When the Romans

A view of Hadrian's Wall spanning the countryside of Northumberland, England.

MACBETH

One of the most villainous and tragic characters in literature is the title character of Shakespeare's *Macbeth*. In the play, Macbeth, thane (lord) of Cawdor, murders his guest, King Duncan I, encouraged by his venomous wife. He is then, in turn, killed by Malcolm, Duncan's son.

Macbeth is based on historical fact, but the facts are far different from those in the drama. The real Macbeth was a grandson of King Kenneth III, who had been murdered by Duncan, and hence had a legitimate claim to the throne. Macbeth did kill Duncan, but it was not as he slept in bed, as Shakespeare wrote, but in a pitched battle in A.D. 1040.

In the play, Macbeth, after only a short time, is killed by Malcolm in a duel. The real Macbeth ruled for seventeen years and by most accounts was a wise and respected king. He made a pilgrimage to Rome in A.D. 1050 and, according to one chronicle, as quoted in *Scotland: A Concise History* by Fitzroy Maclean, "scattered money among the poor like seed."

Macbeth was, indeed, killed by Malcolm in battle, but Macbeth's stepson Lulach was made king. When Lulach was killed a year later, Malcolm took the throne.

abandoned Britain about 450, the Romanized Britons were easy prey for the invading Germanic tribes, the Angles, Saxons, and Jutes. The fierce Caledonians fighting from their mountain strongholds were more successful at resistance. Scotland thus remained essentially a Celtic country while the land south of the wall became Anglo-Saxon England.

Scotland, however, was not yet Scotland. The Gaelic word for the country was Alba, and it was still Caledonia to the rest of the world. Five peoples would eventually merge to form the nation: the Britons, the Picts, the Angles, the Scots, and the Norsemen.

At the time of the Roman withdrawal, the strongest group in Scotland were the Picts, a mysterious people of uncertain origin who ruled everything north of the Firth of Forth. While they most likely had some Celtic ancestry, they spoke a completely different language from their neighbors and their carvings suggest a Middle Eastern origin. Their name, meaning "painted ones," was coined by the Romans because their warriors were painted or tattooed. No one knows what they called themselves.

South of the Picts in the region of the Clyde, allied tribes of Britons ruled an area referred to as the kingdom of Strathclyde. At first the Britons ruled the entire southern part of Scotland, but later (in around 550) they were ousted from the southwest or Lothian region by the Angles, one of the three invading Germanic tribes. The Angles established the kingdom of Northumbria, extending from the Firth of Forth far into northeast England.

THE SCOTS

The Scots were the fourth major population group, a tribe originating in northern Ireland. Some old Roman maps, in fact, label the northern part of Ireland, "Scotia." The Scots began migrating to extreme southwestern Scotland in the third century, but it was not until 500 that Fergus MacErc and his brothers Angus and Lorne arrived with a sizeable force and the Scots' area expanded. At first their holdings did not constitute a Scottish kingdom but were part of the kingdom of Dalriada, ruled from Ireland.

The four groups (the Norsemen came later) were in almost constant conflict, both among each other and within themselves. Christianity was the principal factor that forged them into a nation. Scattered Christian communities almost certainly existed in Scotland from Roman times. The first recorded missionary was a native of Strathclyde, Saint Ninian, who established a monastery at Whithorn on the Solway Firth about 397 and sent monks to convert the Picts, but with little success.

The abbey on the island of Iona, off the west coast of Scotland. The abbey was founded by Irish missionary Saint Columba in 563.

Missionaries from Ireland, arriving later, were much more successful. Chief among these was Saint Columba, who established an abbey on the tiny western island of Iona in 563. From there, he and his disciples spread throughout the country, converting the Britons and Picts. Columba himself traveled to the Pictish capital at Inverness, supposedly defeating a monster at Loch Ness along the way, and converted the king. One of his disciples, Saint Adian, converted the Angles of Northumbria.

Dalriada had already been converted by other Irish missionaries, chiefly Saint Oran in the 540s, but Columba still had great influence in the kingdom. When he first arrived at Iona, the Scots were in danger of being overcome by the still-pagan Picts. Columba consolidated the warring factions and consolidated the monarchy. By the time he died in A.D. 597 Scottish Dalriada was a strong, independent kingdom.

POLITICAL UNION

Before another hundred years had passed, all four kingdoms had been Christianized, and the political union was not far off. The Picts remained the strongest of the four, and their victory over the Angles at Nechtansmere in 685 cut off, for the time being, any further Anglo-Saxon encroachment into Scotland. The Picts and Scots were united in 843 when Kenneth McAlpin, king of the Scots, ascended the throne of the Picts. His claim was vague, perhaps through marriage, but he was aided by the fact that the Picts had been weakened by a new enemy—the Norsemen.

Kenneth McAlpin, considered the founder of the Scottish kingdom.

The Norsemen had begun raiding the British coast in 789 and soon had set up colonies in coastal areas throughout Britain and Ireland. Throughout the 800s they conquered first the Shetland and Orkney Islands, then the Hebrides off the west coast, and finally occupied the Caithness and Sutherland areas at the extreme north of the mainland.

Kenneth McAlpin made no attempt to oust the Norsemen, but instead devoted his energies to attempting to conquer the Angles of Lothian. He failed but is still considered the first king of Scotland; his descendants ruled the country for the next five hundred years. The medieval Huntingdon Chronicle referred to him as "the first of the Scots to obtain the monarchy of all of Albania [Alba], which is now called Scotia."[3] The Scots, an Irish tribe, had now given their name to the entire area. An enduring mystery of Scotland is that the Picts, for centuries the strongest people, were submerged, their language and culture disappearing.

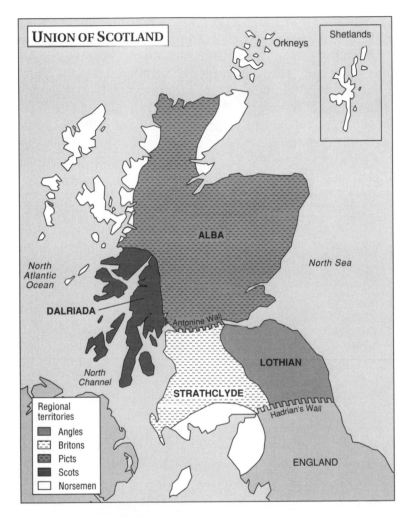

UNION OF SCOTLAND

Orkneys

Shetlands

ALBA

North Sea

North
Atlantic
Ocean

DALRIADA

Antonine Wall

LOTHIAN

North
Channel

STRATHCLYDE

Hadrian's Wall

Regional
territories

- Angles
- Britons
- Picts
- Scots
- Norsemen

ENGLAND

MCALPIN'S SUCCESSORS

It was left to Kenneth McAlpin's successors to further unify
Scotland. They partially succeeded in 1018 when King
Malcolm II finally defeated the Angles and absorbed Lothian. In that same year Malcolm managed to install his
grandson, Duncan, as king of Strathclyde. When Malcolm
died in 1034, Duncan became king of all of Scotland except for the Norsemen's area. It would not be until 1266
that Norway sold the Western Isles to Scotland and 1432
before the Orkney and Shetland Islands became Scottish.
Thus it was that the fifth major ethnic group—the Norse—
left a rich cultural heritage, but only in limited areas of the
north and west.

With the absorption of the Norse territories, the peopling of Scotland was essentially completed. There would be another major cultural and historical influence from outside— the Normans, who successfully invaded England from France in 1066—but the ethnic pattern of Scotland had been established as a mixture of Celtic, English, and Norse. Scotland had achieved unity, but its battles for independence were just beginning.

THE MONARCHY

By the year 1034 Scotland had essentially taken shape, with Scots, Britons, Picts, and Angles welded into one kingdom. The Norman invasion of England, however, would soon introduce a new and enduring phase in Scottish history, one in which the Scots would find themselves alternately losing their independence to and winning it back from their larger, more powerful neighbor. The Scottish monarchy would ultimately survive, but only by merging with that of England.

The merging with England began soon after the unification of Scotland. Malcolm III, known as Canmore, or "Big Head," had been raised in England during the reign of Macbeth, who had killed Malcolm's father, Duncan. Malcolm's second wife, Margaret, was an English princess who had fled to Scotland after the invasion of the Normans. Between them, Malcolm and Margaret began to introduce foreign ideas such as feudalism—a system under which nobles held land from the king in exchange for military service—and church practices more in line with Rome than the old Celtic Christian church. Under Margaret's guidance, the Scottish court became more refined and Scots replaced Gaelic as the court language.

Malcolm had ambitions of expanding his kingdom into northern England and undertook a series of raids across the border. Goaded into action, William "the Conquerer," the Norman duke who had successfully invaded England, invaded Scotland as well. In 1071 he forced Malcolm to swear allegiance to him, the first of many times a Scottish king would be forced into obedience by an English monarch.

After Malcolm was killed in 1093, four of his sons ruled in turn. The last and by far the most able was David I, king from 1124 to 1153. Like his father, David had been brought up in England where, according to the chronicler William of Malmesbury, his manners "were polished from the rust of Scottish barbarity."[4] After becoming king, he distributed large estates to some of his Norman friends. Some of the most powerful and important names in Scottish history—Bruce, Frasar, Gordon, Balliol—derive from these Norman newcomers.

DAVID'S REFORMS

Under David I the feudal system begun by his father took firm root. Likewise, the church was reformed on the English model with a system of bishops. Many abbeys and monasteries were built and richly endowed. David appointed sheriffs and "justiciars," somewhat similar to justices of the peace, to keep law and order; and he established the first Royal Council, a body of advisers that would eventually develop into the Scottish Parliament.

Perhaps David's most lasting and important innovations were in the field of commerce. He encouraged foreign trade. He set up two royal mints to coin money and also established a uniform system of weights and measures. Even more significant, he established market towns on the English model called "burghs," the most important of which was Edinburgh. When David died in 1153, Lowland Scotland had been brought within the English sphere of influence and much of the old Celtic way of life had vanished. In the Highlands, however, the old ways still were followed and the wild clansmen paid little heed to the king far to the south.

King David I initiated many reforms in Scotland based on English models.

David was succeeded by a grandson, Malcolm IV, a boy of 11, under whose weak rule King Henry II of England forced Scotland to return Northumbria, which had been won by David. Fortunately for Scotland, Malcolm died young in 1165 and was succeeded by his much abler brother, William I, known as William the Lion because of his courage. William's emblem, a raging lion, remains the royal symbol of Scotland.

THE AULD ALLIANCE

William wanted Northumbria back and was prepared to invade England to get it. Henry II and the king of France were enemies, so William made an alliance with France in 1165. This connection would endure through the centuries, with Scotland and France combining against England in what would be known as the "Auld Alliance." This time, at least, the alliance did Scotland little good. William's invasion of England in 1174 failed, and he was taken prisoner and forced to sign the Treaty of Falaise under which Scotland became a feudal fief, or subject territory, of England and the Scottish church was placed under the rule of English archbishops.

Scotland regained its independence in 1189 when Henry II's son, Richard I "the Lionheart," restored it in exchange for a gift of money with which to mount a crusade to Palestine. Three years later Pope Celestine III released the Scottish church from England and placed it under the direct control of Rome.

Scotland and England were mostly at peace for the next hundred years, but there were enemies elsewhere. William the Lion's son and grandson, Alexander II and Alexander III, turned their attention to the Gaelic chiefs in the west, whose allegiance was to Norway but who in reality were completely independent. In 1263 King Hakon of Norway, reacting to raids by Alexander III into his territory, assembled a large invasion fleet. A storm in the Firth of Clyde damaged many of the ships, and the troops who made it to shore were defeated. The Norwegians then signed a treaty in 1266 that gave all of western Scotland, including the Hebrides Islands, to Alexander. Only the Orkney and Shetland island groups remained to Norway.

Celestine III, pope from 1191 to 1198.

A TIME OF WAR

When Alexander III was killed in a riding accident in 1286, the era of peace and security in Scotland ended and centuries of internal strife and war with England ensued. Alexander's only direct heir was a four-year-old granddaughter, Margaret the "Maid of Norway," whose father was the king of Norway and who remained there temporarily while a council ruled in her name. The king of England, Edward I, wanted to incorporate Scotland into his kingdom and arranged a marriage between his son and Margaret. His plans went awry when Margaret died on a voyage to Scotland in 1290.

With Margaret's death the royal line of Malcolm Canmore ended and several claimants for the throne came forward. The two with the best claims were John Balliol and Robert Bruce, both descended from daughters of a younger brother of William the Lion.

The Bishop of Saint Andrew's, fearing a civil war, suggested that Edward of England be asked to make the decision

BRUCE AND THE SPIDER

According to legend, Robert the Bruce, in summoning up the will to rebound from defeat and win freedom for Scotland, drew upon the example of a spider.

Bruce was crowned king of Scotland at Scone in 1306, but many Scottish nobles were against him as was King Edward I of England. Edward invaded Scotland and defeated Bruce in battles at Methven and Dalry. Bruce's wife was imprisoned, and three of his brothers were executed. Bruce escaped and went into hiding, moving from place to place in the Western Isles to escape the pursuing English.

As the story goes, he finally took refuge in a cave on the remote island of Rathlin off the coast of northern Ireland. He was so despondent that he thought about abandoning his vision for Scotland, but then he saw a spider struggling to spin a web at the cave entrance. Just as the web would near completion, it would be knocked down by the wind. Still the spider persisted and after many tries completed the web, which was able to withstand the gale.

Bruce supposedly took hope from the spider and vowed to make the attempt to regain his throne. He returned to Scotland, quietly and slowly built up a following, and in 1314 routed King Edward II of England at the Battle of Bannockburn to win independence for his country.

from among the rivals. Little did he realize what he had let Scotland in for. Edward, to be known to history as the "Hammer of the Scots," accepted, but viewed his role not as a judge, but as a feudal lord over Scotland. Accordingly, he chose Balliol, an ineffective man nicknamed Toom Tabard, or "empty coat," whom he thought he could easily dominate.

When Edward demanded that Balliol contribute heavily to England's wars in France, Balliol was sufficiently insulted to resist and in 1295 renewed Scotland's alliance with France. Edward reacted swiftly, marching north and rallying the Scottish nobles loyal to him, including Balliol's rival, Robert Bruce. His troops defeated those of Balliol at Dunbar, Balliol renounced the crown, and Edward forced thousands of nobles and landowners to sign the "Ragman's Roll," a document acknowledging him as king. He then returned to London, bearing with him the ancient Stone of Scone, used for centuries as the seat of Scottish kings when they were crowned.

WILLIAM WALLACE

Scotland was a defeated nation, but rebellion was not far off. In 1297 a young Scottish noble named William Wallace killed the Sheriff of Lanark, who had executed Wallace's wife for helping him to escape following his arrest after a brawl with some English soldiers. Wallace quickly went from being an outlaw to being the leader of a rebellion. When English troops under the Earl of Surrey moved against him, Wallace

A statue of Scottish rebel leader William Wallace in the Borders region of southeast Scotland.

Robert the Bruce and his second wife. Bruce, who reigned from 1306 to 1329, liberated Scotland from English rule in 1314.

and his forces soundly defeated them at Stirling Bridge. The next year Wallace was defeated by Edward himself at Falkirk. Wallace escaped, but the resistance was broken. He was eventually captured in 1305 and executed.

But the flame of rebellion was far from extinguished. In 1306 Robert Bruce, grandson of Balliol's rival, decided to make a bid for the throne. Although he is ranked as perhaps Scotland's greatest hero, Bruce was infamous in his time as untrustworthy, always ready to change sides if he thought it would work in his favor. A good example was the meeting he arranged with his chief rival, John Comyn. Although the meeting was in a church, possibly as a safeguard against treachery, Bruce stabbed Comyn to death.

Even though he was excommunicated, or cut off from the church, for this murder, Bruce had himself crowned king in a ceremony at Scone; but he was unable to unite the country behind him, and his army was destroyed by the English near Perth.

Bruce spent a year in hiding, then gathered another army, defeating the English at Loudon Hill. Edward tried to take the field in person, but he died on the march northward in 1307 and was succeeded by his inept son, Edward II. Bruce took advantage of Edward II's troubles with his own nobles to capture several English strongholds over the next few years. When Edward finally led his army to put down the rebellion in 1314, he was put to flight and his troops slaughtered or captured at the Battle of Bannockburn on June 24.

BANNOCKBURN'S EFFECTS

This victory, which took place only a few hundred yards from the site of Wallace's victory seventeen years earlier, was a major milestone in Scottish history. While it did not bring a lasting peace between Scotland and England, it guaranteed that Scotland would no longer be ruled by an English king. When, centuries later, the countries were united, it would be first as two nations with a single king and later as a united kingdom.

While border clashes dragged on for years, England never again mounted a major invasion. In 1320 the Scottish nobility and clergy sent to Pope John XXII the Declaration of Abroath, Scotland's version of the American Declaration of Independence. It asked for recognition as an independent nation and said, in part,

> As long as 100 of us remain alive, we will never in any way be forced to tolerate the rule of the English. Because we do not fight for glory, or riches, or honors, but for freedom alone, which no good man gives up except with his life.[5]

Four years later the pope recognized Bruce as king, and in 1328, with the Treaty of Northampton, England formally recognized Scotland's independence.

Bruce died in 1329, but Scotland's independence endured despite having, time and again, an infant monarch fought over by factions of the nobility. Nor was conflict with England at an end. In 1339 the warlike Edward III, who succeeded his unfortunate father, embarked on a series of wars with France that was to last until 1453 and go down in history as the Hundred Years' War. In 1346, after a disastrous defeat at Crécy, the French called on their traditional Scottish allies for help. David II, Bruce's son but nowhere near his father's equal, invaded England but was

Robert the Bruce reviews his troops before the Battle of Bannockburn. The June 24, 1314 battle was a major victory for Scotland.

defeated at Neville's Cross and taken prisoner. He spent the next twelve years in idle luxury at the English court while Scotland was ruled in his name by Robert Stewart, son of Bruce's daughter, Margery.

THE STEWARTS

Although independent, Scotland was in a poor way. When David died without an heir in 1371, Stewart took the throne as Robert II, first of the Stewart line of kings. Neither he nor his son, Robert III, were strong enough to prevent violent conflict among their nobles. As one chronicler wrote,

> There was no law in Scotland; but the great man oppressed the poor man and the whole country was one den of thieves. Slaughters, robberies, fire-raising [ar-

THE BLACK DINNER

Medieval Scotland was often characterized by barbarity, cruelty, and treachery among the factious nobility. The Spanish ambassador, Pedro de Ayala, is quoted in *Scotland: A Concise History* as writing, "They spend all their time in wars, and when there are no wars they fight one another."

A prime example was the rivalry between Sir William Crichton, regent for the young James II, and the powerful Douglas family. In 1440 Crichton decided to break the power of the Douglases. Pretending to want to settle the conflict, he invited the earl of Douglas, a boy of fourteen, and his younger brother to dine with the king.

Toward the end of the meal, a large covered tray was set before the Douglases. The cover was taken off to reveal the head of a black bull, a symbol of death. The young earl and his brother were seized, accused of treason, and beheaded in the nine-year-old king's presence.

The event is known in Scottish history as the Black Dinner, and followers of the Douglases immortalized it in this poem (from *Scotland: A Concise History*):

> Edinburg Castle, towne and toure [tower],
>
> Good grant thae sink for sinne!
>
> And that even for the black dinoir
>
> Earl Douglas got therein.

son] and other crimes went unpunished, and justice was sent into banishment, beyond the kingdom's bounds.[6]

Fortunes began to rise in 1424 with Robert III's son, James I, who already had been king eighteen years, but had been a prisoner in England. He was able to return to Scotland when England, facing military trouble in France, sought peace with its northern neighbor.

James was an energetic man, determined, he said, to make "the key keep the castle and the bracken-bush the cow."[7] In other words, he wanted to take control of the warring nobles and bring peace and security to his people. He introduced a series of measures to foster law and order and to curb the power of the nobles. He raised new taxes and reformed the financial system, appointing a royal treasurer. His reforms brought him into conflict with the nobles, who assassinated him in 1437.

James I strove to reduce the power and conflicts of the nobles.

The next two kings, James II and James III, both began their rules as children; their reigns were marked by renewed warfare between rival nobles. The Douglas family was especially strong, ruling southwest Scotland as if it were a separate kingdom. For fifty years the Douglases and those nobles around the kings fought for power. An all-too-typical event occurred in 1440 when the young James II's chief adviser, Sir William Crichton, had the young earl of Douglas and his younger brother murdered during a dinner. Twelve years later, James invited another earl of Douglas to dinner and stabbed him to death despite a promise of safe conduct.

JAMES IV

A strong monarchy was re-established by James IV, who came to the throne in 1488. Well-educated and cultured, he brought to Scotland the Renaissance, a rebirth of classical learning that had begun in Italy about a hundred years earlier. James founded universities, including a medical college, and improved the legal system. He encouraged the arts, and there was a flowering of Scots poetry.

THE COURT OF JAMES IV

King James IV, who ascended the throne in 1488, was the most successful and popular of the Stewart rulers of Scotland. In *Scotland: A Concise History*, Spain's ambassador Pedro de Ayala describes the king as having, "a wonderful force of intellect, an incredible knowledge of all things."

Under his leadership the Scottish court was transformed from a rough, almost barbaric place into one of refinement. Literature and the arts flourished as the Renaissance, which had begun in Italy around the end of the fourteenth century, finally reached Scotland.

Still, Scotland was poor compared to the other nations of Europe. In one of his dispatches, which appears in *The Land and People of Scotland*, de Ayala writes,

> The people are handsome. They like foreigners so much that they dispute with one another as to who shall have and treat a foreigner in his house. They are vain and ostentatious by nature. They spend all they have to keep up appearances. They are as well dressed as it is possible for such a country as that in which they live. They are courageous, strong, quick, agile. They are envious to excess. . . . The kingdom is very old and very noble . . . not rich; the fault of which is not owing to the land. But on the other hand they are not so poor but that they live as well as others who are much richer; only they have nothing to put into their strongboxes.

James made a brilliant marriage, wedding Margaret Tudor, daughter of King Henry VII of England in 1502, a marriage that was to have enormous implications later in the century. The two countries signed a treaty vowing "perpetual peace" that year, but the peace lasted only eleven years. James had tried to maintain a balance between England and France, but when Henry attacked France in 1513, James attacked England in recognition of the Auld Alliance. It was a disaster. The two armies met at Flodden, and the Scots were routed. Most of their chief nobles, including King James, were killed.

Once more Scotland had a boy king, James V. The nobles were divided between two factions, one wanting to maintain the French alliance, the other favoring closer connection with England. Religion was at the heart of the split. Protestantism was sweeping Europe—and England was Protestant while France was Catholic. James eventually sided with France and Catholicism, even though many of his subjects had become Protestants, and took as his second wife Marie de Guise, daughter of a French duke. King Henry VIII of England, determined to claim Scotland for Protestantism, invaded in 1542 and defeated James's troops at Solway Moss. Two weeks later James died, some said of a broken spirit. The new ruler of Scotland was a week-old daughter, Mary Queen of Scots.

Henry VIII invaded Scotland again in 1544 and his troops were so brutal that Scottish nobles, both Catholic and Protestant, united against him and turned to France for help. Young Mary was sent to France for safety and in 1558 was married to the heir to the French throne. Meanwhile, Marie de Guise, the Scottish queen's mother, ruled Scotland in her daughter's name, filling all important government posts with Frenchmen.

KNOX AND PROTESTANTISM

It began to appear as if France, not England, would absorb Scotland, but religion was to tear the Auld Alliance apart. The Catholic church in Scotland was notably corrupt, with some priests barely able to read and others living openly with mistresses and children. Bishops and abbots grew rich while the common people were as poor as ever. Resentment against the church grew, and with it resentment against the French.

Fanning the flames of discontent was John Knox, a radical Protestant who thundered against the French in general and Marie de Guise in particular. In 1557 a group of powerful Protestant nobles calling themselves the Lords of the Congregation had signed a document eventually known as the First Covenant vowing to establish a new national church. Marie de Guise tried to suppress the Covenanters by force, but Knox, who had been in self-imposed exile in Europe, returned to Scotland in 1559. Under the spell of his inflammatory sermons, mobs broke into Catholic churches, smashing altars.

Protestant leader John Knox reproves the Catholic Scottish queen Mary in 1563. Knox led Parliament to ban Catholicism in Scotland.

Marie de Guise sought and received help from France, but the Protestant lords of Scotland found an unlikely ally in England, the ancient enemy, but now ruled by the Protestant queen Elizabeth I. Elizabeth was reluctant to interfere in Scotland but even more wary of a French takeover. The English fleet blocked a French invasion, and when Marie de Guise died in 1560, the French withdrew. Queen Mary, eighteen years old and newly widowed, was allowed to return to Scotland. She was permitted to worship in private as a Catholic, but Parliament, led by Knox, banned the Catholic church and established the Church of Scotland.

MARY QUEEN OF SCOTS

Mary Queen of Scots is one of the most tragic figures in Scottish history, but her fate was largely of her own making. Catholic queen of a now fiercely Protestant country, her rule was complicated by the fact that, as the granddaughter of

THE DEATH OF DARNLEY

The death of Henry Stewart, Lord Darnley, remains one of the most dramatic and mysterious events in Scottish history. It was especially significant since it led to the downfall of his wife, Mary Queen of Scots.

The two had been married only a few months when Darnley's true nature showed itself. Outwardly handsome, he was arrogant and boorish. He spent most of his time drinking with equally disreputable companions and consorting with prostitutes. However, when Mary grew close to her Italian secretary, David Riccio, Darnley was insanely jealous.

One night in March 1566, as Mary and Riccio sat in her apartments in Holyrood Palace in Edinburgh, a group of Darnley's friends burst in and stabbed Riccio to death before her eyes as Darnley waited outside.

Later Darnley tried to deny his part in the murder, but his friends had written proof. Mary pretended to forgive him and, the next year, sent him to a small house in nearby Kirk o' Field to recover from an illness. Late one night a tremendous explosion leveled the house and Darnley was killed. It appeared at first to be an accident, but an examination of the body showed that he had been strangled.

The murder, and Mary's subsequent elopement with James Hepburn, earl of Bothwell, turned all factions in Scotland against Mary. She was forced to give up the throne and eventually escaped to England, only to be kept prisoner by her cousin, Queen Elizabeth I, until she was beheaded in 1587.

Henry Stewart, Lord Darnley, second husband of Mary Queen of Scots.

King Henry VII of England, she was now next in line to the English throne should Elizabeth die without an heir.

Mary's choice of a new husband led to her undoing. In 1565 she married a cousin, Henry Stewart, Lord Darnley, who proved to be thoroughly worthless, treating Mary shamefully and infuriating her Protestant advisers. In 1565, pregnant but disgusted by Darnley, Mary found friendship in her Italian secretary, David Riccio; and love in the dashing and Protestant James Hepburn, earl of Bothwell. After the jealous Darnley and a group of friends murdered Riccio in Mary's presence, Bothwell arranged, probably with Mary's knowledge, to have Darnley killed. Two months later, now the mother of an infant son, Mary allowed herself to be abducted by Bothwell and married him in a Protestant service.

By allowing her heart to overcome her better judgment, Mary had scandalized Scotland, and Scotland turned against her. Taken by force from Bothwell, who was made to flee the country, she was paraded through the streets of Edinburgh

Mary Queen of Scots caused an uproar among the Scottish people with her scandalous second marriage.

The flag of Great Britain combined the English cross of Saint George and the Scottish cross of Saint Andrew.

in a red petticoat, symbolizing adultery, and was forced to renounce the throne in favor of her baby son, James VI. She was imprisoned but in 1568 escaped to England and threw herself on the mercy of her cousin Elizabeth. Mary would remain a virtual prisoner for nineteen years until, convicted in one of many plots against Elizabeth's life, she was executed in 1587.

UNION OF CROWNS

King James VI, who barely knew his mother, made only a token protest at her execution. He now was the heir to Elizabeth (who had never married) and did not want to do anything to risk losing the English crown. He remained in close contact with Robert Cecil, Elizabeth's chief adviser, who was determined that the succession would be smooth. When Elizabeth died in 1603, King James VI of Scotland also became King James I of England.

Scotland had emerged from more than five hundred years of conflict with England to the threshold of unity. James referred to his twin kingdoms as "Great Britain," and they had a common flag, the Union Jack combining the English cross of Saint George and the Scottish cross of Saint Andrew. The two kingdoms still were separate, and would remain so for another century, but the foundation for complete union had been laid.

4

UNION AND
THEREAFTER

With the ascension of James VI of Scotland to the throne of England, the two countries had a single king but still were separate nations with a long history of conflict. Another century would pass before they would be truly united, and yet another 150 years before the religious question finally was settled and Scotland able to reach full flower as a modern, economically viable nation.

Although Scotland had officially become Protestant in 1560, the issue of church governance was far from settled. James favored an episcopal system, one governed by bishops appointed by the monarch, rather than a presbyterian system in which the national church ruled itself through an elected body independent of the throne. Some extreme Protestants wanted to do away with the monarchy and have the presbyters, or elected leaders of the church, govern the entire nation. Still others wanted individual congregations to have complete authority independent of anyone, presbyters or bishops.

Before becoming king of England as well as of Scotland, James played a very careful political game, needing to maintain the support of the national church—called the Kirk. Once he was more secure, he allowed free rein to his belief in the divine right and authority of kings. In 1610 he abolished the so-called Golden Act of 1592 that had abolished bishops. Eight years later he forced the Five Articles of Perth through the church's General Assembly, which restored some banned practices, such as receiving Holy Communion, kneeling instead of standing, and celebrating Christmas and other festivals. Many Scots refused to obey, walking miles to attend unlawful outdoor services rather than go to "kneeling churches." James wisely did not have the Five Articles rigorously enforced.

CHARLES I

James's son and successor in 1625, Charles I, was even more devoted to traditional church ceremony and episcopal government, but he lacked his father's political sense. Although born in Scotland Charles did not bother to return there until 1633, seven years after his father's death, to be officially crowned. The ceremony was in Saint Giles, Edinburgh, which Charles designated a cathedral for the occasion, complete with a new bishop. He was accompanied by Archbishop Laud of Canterbury, suspected by many of wanting to return England—and Scotland—to Catholicism.

Scotland grumbled, but the grumbling exploded into violence in 1637 when Charles attempted to supplant the prayer book of John Knox with one written by Laud. When a priest attempted to read from the new book at Saint Giles, a woman named Jenny Geddes reacted by throwing a stool at him. A shower of missiles followed, and the priest was forced to flee from the pulpit.

King James VI of Scotland firmly believed in the divine right of kings and favored an episcopal church system.

Where his father might have pulled back, Charles was stubborn. He ordered all who protested the new book to submit to his will. Rather than do so, several hundred people representing all social levels met in 1638 at Greyfriars Church in Edinburgh to sign a National Covenant vowing to resist all attempts to overthrow the Kirk. An army was raised and Charles, to get money to raise an army of his own, was forced to call on the English Parliament, which he had dissolved years before. Parliament was dominated by Protestants called Puritans because of their desire to purify the church from all Catholic remnants.

The conflict between Charles and his English Parliament erupted into civil war in 1642. The Scots tried not to take sides, but they feared that a royal victory in England might mean the end of the Kirk in Scotland. A Scottish army fought alongside Parliament's forces. When it was apparent that Charles was losing the war, he abruptly surrendered to the Scots in 1646, hoping to reach an agreement with them and win their support. When he refused to acknowledge Presbyterianism, however, the Scots turned him over to the English, who imprisoned and finally executed him in 1649.

CROMWELL

The Scots, who still felt strong affection for their Stewart monarchs, declared Charles's son, Charles II, king. They knew that the English leader, Oliver Cromwell, was no friend to Presbyterianism. Cromwell promptly invaded and in 1651 the last Scottish army to fight an English army was defeated at Worcester. Charles managed to avoid capture and fled to France.

Cromwell ruled both England and Scotland, but when he died in 1658 the Scots were instrumental in restoring Charles II to the throne. Charles promptly broke all his promises to support the Presbyterians, restoring the bishops and declaring that "Presbytery was not a religion for gentlemen."[8] Many Presbyterians grudgingly accepted Charles's edicts, but the more radical "Covenanters" refused to attend the bishops'

After Charles I was executed in 1649, Oliver Cromwell became leader of England and Scotland. Here, Cromwell opens Charles's coffin to view the body.

churches and even staged a brief rebellion, which was savagely crushed. This split between Scottish Protestants would eventually result in the formation of the Free Church of Scotland, a branch separate from the Kirk.

The persecution of Protestants reached a peak in the early 1680s, led by Charles's brother James, a Catholic. Those who refused to swear an oath against the Covenant were executed on the spot by English troops during what was known in Scotland as the "Killing Time." In 1688, three years after he succeeded his brother on the throne, James (who had made himself equally unpopular in England) was forced to flee to France. The English, with near unanimous support from the Scots, gave the crown to William of Orange, husband of James's eldest daughter Mary. William, a staunch Protestant, removed the Scottish bishops and finally gave the Kirk its independence.

Still, peace remained elusive. The Highlands had never been completely brought under the control of the central government, and the Highland clans were a source of discontent. Many clan chiefs, some of them still staunchly Catholic, longed for the return of James, their "king over the water." Called Jacobites for the French version of the name James, they briefly rebelled in 1689 in support of James's unsuccessful invasion of Ireland.

THE GLENCOE MASSACRE

In 1691 William required all clan chiefs to sign an oath of loyalty to him by January 1, 1692. Anyone who refused would be stripped of all possessions. When the date came all but two had signed. One of these, MacIan MacDonald of Glencoe, signed three days late. William decided to make an example of him. On his orders troops of the rival Campbells fell on the unsuspecting MacDonalds, slaughtering thirty-eight men, women, and children, most as they slept. The Glencoe Massacre did much to deepen the discontent of the Highlanders.

The Lowlands were not completely content, either. The union of the crowns had not brought economic prosperity to Scotland. On the contrary, many merchants claimed that all the trade advantages were with the English and that they could not look to King William or the English Parliament for relief. The feeling grew that Scotland would be better off if it

THE GLENCOE MASSACRE

Of all the brutal deeds in Scottish history the massacre of the MacDonalds of Glencoe in 1692 stands out. Even though carried out by Scots against their own countrymen, it was ordered by the English and remained for generations a source of bitterness.

When King William III of England ordered the Highland chiefs to sign an oath of loyalty to him by January 1, MacIan MacDonald of Glencoe was three days late in so doing. William's secretary of state for Scotland, John Dalrymple, chose to make an example of the MacDonalds and received the king's signed permission.

On February 1, a company of soldiers commanded by Captain Robert Campbell was quartered in Glencoe with the MacDonalds, ostensibly to collect taxes. Despite the fact that the Campbells and MacDonalds were hereditary enemies, old MacIan was hospitable toward the officer and his troops, drinking with them and playing cards far into the winter nights.

On February 12 Campbell received a message (which appears in *Scotland: A Concise History*): "You are hereby ordered to fall upon the MacDonalds of Glencoe and put all to the sword under seventy; you are to have a special care that the old fox [MacIan] and his sons do on no account escape your hands."

Before dawn the next morning, Campbell's troops fell on their unsuspecting hosts, moving from house to house and killing the MacDonalds as they slept. MacIan was shot, as was his wife. A soldier cut off her dead fingers to get at her rings. In all, thirty-eight MacDonalds died, but some escaped into the mountains.

The Glencoe Massacre, although successful in the short term in cowing the Highlanders, added much to the legacy of bitterness and distrust of the English and would be a rallying point in the Jacobite uprisings of the next century. As for the perpetrators of the massacre, Dalrymple eventually became an earl while Campbell was promoted to colonel.

were joined with England under a single Parliament, one in which Scottish voices would be heard.

The idea of political union with England was wildly unpopular with most Scots. When the Act of Union was proposed in 1706, riots broke out in major cities. As was usual with the Scots, the opposition was divided within itself. Some in the Scottish Parliament were reassured when an Act of Security was added guaranteeing the freedom of the Kirk. Other members, it was widely believed, had been bribed. In January 1707, while a mob outside protested, the Scottish Parliament approved the Act of Union by a vote of 110 to 69.

After the union was approved in London, the Scottish Parliament met on March 25 for what would be the last time in almost three hundred years. The royal crown and the sword and scepter of state were wrapped in linen, removed to Edinburgh Castle, and locked away. "There's ane end of ane auld sang," said one Scottish lord sadly.[9] Scotland had ceased to exist as a nation and was now part of the United Kingdom.

"THE '15"

The Act of Union did nothing to quench the Jacobite spirit of the Highlands. When Queen Anne, James II's younger daughter, died in 1714, the Stewart line of monarchs ended and the throne went to George I of Hanover in Germany, a great-grandson of James I. The Jacobites immediately proclaimed James II's son, James Edward, as king, raised an army and launched a rebellion,

The Campbells attack the MacDonalds at the Glencoe Massacre on February 13, 1692. Thirty-eight people were killed in the slaughter.

The Jacobite museum at Glenfinnan. The Jacobites supported Stewart heir "Bonnie Prince Charlie."

known as "The '15" for the year 1715. Even before James Edward could come over from France, however, the army was crushed by government troops in the Battle of Sheriffmuir. James Edward, known to history as "The Old Pretender," arrived in Scotland the next month but shortly thereafter returned to France, never to return.

After the rebellion, the government took steps to bring the Highlands under control. Forts were constructed, and roads were built to expedite troop movements. Still unvanquished, the Highland Jacobites rose one last time in 1745. This time their leader was James II's grandson Charles Edward Stewart, "The Young Pretender" or, as he is better known, "Bonnie Prince Charlie."

The prince landed in the Hebrides in July accompanied by only seven followers and proclaimed himself king. His chances of success were so slim that even some of the most ardent Jacobites urged him to go home. He replied simply, "I am come home."[10] Charles raised his standard at Glenfinnan in August, and the clansmen rallied to his cause. Against all odds his army swept across Scotland. More and more Scots joined him. In September his army captured Edinburgh and routed a government army at Prestonpans.

Charles next invaded England. He knew he did not have the military strength to defeat the full English army, but he hoped that the French would intervene in his behalf. They did not. The Scots marched as far south as Derby, 130 miles from London, then turned back. When Charles reached Scotland once more, his forces were weakened by desertion, and government forces were massing.

CULLODEN

The end came on April 16, 1746, on the moor of Culloden near Inverness. The wild Highland charge that had prevailed at Prestonpans withered before the massed musketry of the English, who were led by the Duke of Cumberland, a son of King George II. "Butcher" Cumberland showed no mercy.

THE DARIEN ADVENTURE

The 1600s saw a great expansion of European colonies around the world. Scotland had two such ventures. The first, a settlement in Nova Scotia (New Scotland) lasted only a few years. The second, at the Isthmus of Darien in Panama, lasted an even shorter time and was a major disaster.

The idea for New Caledonia, as the colony was to be called, was that of William Paterson, a Dumfriesshire businessman. He convinced Scotland's Parliament to create The Company of Scotland Trading to Africa and the Indies and set about raising six hundred thousand pounds, half from Scotland and the rest from England and elsewhere, to finance the colony, which was to make investors rich by moving trade goods back and forth along the narrow strip of land between the Atlantic and Pacific Oceans.

The powerful British East India Company, however, wanted no rivals for investors' money. They convinced King William III to discourage English and Dutch investors. As a result, Scotland bore the entire cost of the venture.

The scheme was doomed from the start. The first expedition in 1698 was completely unprepared for the tropical climate; members took mostly clothing of wool and heavy serge. They faced sweltering heat, disease, and the hostility of Spain, which claimed the area. They appealed for help to English Jamaica, but were told that King William had forbidden it. Two expeditions followed, but all met the same fate. By the time New Caledonia was abandoned late in 1699, more than two thousand people had died and the entire investment had been lost.

The Darien Adventure did have at least one favorable consequence. The Scots were convinced that they could never overcome barriers to foreign trade erected by England and that the only solution lay in a union of the two countries. This thinking was a major factor in the passage of the Act of Union in 1707.

The Darien Adventure was a short-lived Scottish colony in Panama.

FLORA MACDONALD

After Charles Edward Stewart—"Bonnie Prince Charlie"—was defeated at the Battle of Culloden in 1746, he wandered through the western Highlands accompanied by only two or three companions. In the country where he had been proclaimed king he was now a fugitive, hunted night and day by government troops.

He traveled by night, never staying in one place more than a few days. Despite the fact that there was a reward of thirty thousand pounds for his capture, no Highlanders betrayed their prince.

After months on the run, Prince Charles reached the island of South Uist in the Hebrides. While he was trying to arrange for a ship to return him to France, his presence and plight were made known to Flora MacDonald, daughter of a farmer on the island.

At tremendous risk to herself, Flora agreed to help the prince make his way to the Isle of Skye, where a French ship would pick him up. Government troops were combing the Western Isles, so Flora dressed the dashing Stewart prince in the dress of a servant woman, passing him off as her Irish maid, Betty Burke.

The disguise fooled the soldiers, who allowed Flora to take her "maid" on a visit to Skye. In September Charles departed from Skye, never to return to Scotland.

Unfortunately for Flora MacDonald, her part in Charles's escape was discovered. She was arrested and imprisoned in the Tower of London, but was released after a few months. In 1750 she married Allan MacDonald and the couple emigrated to North Carolina in 1774. She returned to Scotland in 1779 and died there in 1790.

Flora MacDonald is revered as one of Scotland's greatest heroines. A statue of her stands before Inverness Castle, only a few miles from the Culloden battlefield. Prince Charles never wrote to her or acknowledged her help in any way.

Flora MacDonald aided Bonnie Prince Charlie's escape from Scotland.

Woodcut depicting the Battle of Culloden, April 16, 1746.

Most of Charles's troops were killed outright; the wounded were shot or bayoneted where they lay. Charles managed to escape—at one point disguised as a lady's maid—and eventually died alone and impoverished in Rome.

The power of the Highland clans had been broken by the Battle of Culloden, the last battle to be fought in the British Isles. Now, the government sought to prevent that power ever from being regained. Chiefs lost their traditional powers. The bearing of arms, especially the great swords known as claymores, was forbidden. Even the wearing of the traditional tartan plaid and the playing of bagpipes were banned on penalty of fine or imprisonment.

The true end of the Highland way of life came when the chiefs, seeking a new source of income, began introducing the hardy Cheviot sheep. The bonds of clan loyalty having been weakened by the English, the chiefs did not hesitate to evict their tenants to make room for these "four footed clansmen." Those forced from the land their ancestors had farmed

THE TARTAN BAN

After the Battle of Culloden, the government took measures designed to weaken the clan system and destroy the traditional way of life in the Highlands. One of the laws prohibited the wearing of the traditional Highland dress, the tartan.

In October of 1751 one John McKay was arrested in Inverness for wearing the outlawed garb. This account of the legal proceeding against him is taken from Invernesshire records and is on display in the Tartan Museum in Inverness:

> John McKay, being interrogated if he or not he had the Tartan plaid and short Tartan Coat which he now wears, upon him when he was apprehended by two of Lord Berry's Regiment now stationed in Inverness the afternoon of this day, judicially acknowledged that he wore the said plaid and Tartan Coat and was seized having both upon him.
>
> The Sheriff finds complaint relevant and proven, and therefore decerns and adjudges the said John McKay to be continued prisoner within the Tollbooth of Inverness, there to remain for the pace of six months from this date, without baill, and grants warrand to and requires the Magistrates of Inverness and Keepers of their Tollbooth to receive and detain him accordingly, and appoints the Clerk of Court to give him an Extract of the Judgement for their Warrand.

The ban on Highland dress was not lifted until 1782. Ironically, kilts and tartans became all the rage throughout both Scotland and England in the 1800s.

for centuries migrated by the thousands to North America and elsewhere. An eyewitness from Skye wrote,

> There were old men and women, too feeble to walk, who were placed in carts; the younger members of the community on foot were carrying the bundles of clothes and household effects, while children with looks of alarm, walked alongside. . . . When they set forth once more, a cry of grief went up to heaven, the long plaintive wail. . . . These people were on their way to be shipped to Canada.[11]

THE SCOTTISH ENLIGHTENMENT

While these "clearances" depopulated the Highlands and virtually ended the old Gaelic way of life, the rest of Scotland prospered after Culloden. The new sense of security in the Lowlands sparked an outpouring of creativity in science, philosophy, and literature that was to last for more than a century and be known as the Scottish Enlightenment. It was an era of innovation—new ways of thinking, new methods of agriculture and manufacturing—and the Scots were primed to take advantage of it. They were far ahead of the rest of Europe in literacy, thanks largely to John Knox's emphasis on universal education, and were also, through the teachings of the Kirk, dedicated to the value of hard work.

Edinburgh became one of the intellectual centers of Europe. Philosopher David Hume pioneered the study of knowledge and how it is acquired. In teaching that people learn more by what they experience and feel intuitively than by external influences, Hume paved the way for much of modern philosophy. Just as influential was Adam Smith, whose *An Inquiry into the Nature and Causes of the Wealth of Nations* in 1776 was the first description of the interplay of government and economics.

Adam Ferguson, another philosopher, emphasized the importance of the interaction of individuals with one another and with groups, laying the foundations of modern sociology. William Robertson revised the writing of history, explaining the influence of material and environmental factors.

Robert Burns, one of Scotland's most beloved poets.

Two giants stood forth in the field of literature—Robert Burns and Walter Scott. Burns, whose chief theme was one of the basic goodness of human nature, wrote chiefly in the Scots language, which was on the verge of extinction. He created a linguistic revival and restored to the Scots a sense of self-respect in being reminded of their heritage. Scott's *Waverley Novels* took a romantic view of history. In addition to building a sense of national pride based on the idealized exploits of Robert Bruce, William Wallace, and other heroes of the past, Scott's works created worldwide interest in Scotland. For the first time, it became fashionable in England to visit Scotland, to have a Scottish ancestor, and

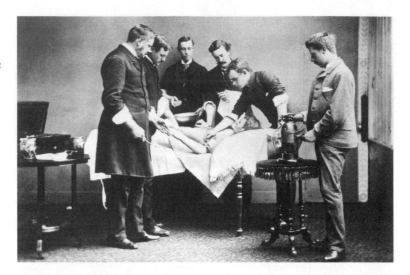

Surgeons perform an operation in Aberdeen, Scotland, in 1870. The discoveries of chloroform and antiseptics by Scots earlier in the century vastly improved surgery.

even to wear a kilt. It was no wonder that David Hume could write in 1757,

> Is it not strange that, at a time when we have lost our Princes, our Parliaments, our independent Government, even the Presence of our chief Nobility, are unhappy in our Accent & Pronunciation, speak a very corrupt Dialect of the Tongue in which we make use of; is it not strange, I say, that in these circumstances, we shou'd really be the People most distinguished for Literature in Europe?[12]

TECHNICAL INNOVATIONS

The Scots are above all, a practical people, inquisitive and good at making things work. The workhorse of the Industrial Revolution was the steam engine developed by a Greenock engineer, James Watt. Communication and travel were improved by the modern road surfaces designed by John Macadam and the bridges and canals built by Thomas Telford and John Rennie. A transplanted Scot, Alexander Graham Bell, would invent the telephone, while a later countryman, John Logie Baird, produced the first working television.

Many of the foremost advances in medicine and science were made in Edinburgh. Joseph Lister's work in antiseptics made surgery vastly safer, while James Simpson's use of chloroform made it painless. A century later another Scot, Alexander Fleming, would furnish a powerful weapon against disease with his discovery of penicillin. In the field of chemistry Joseph Black discovered carbon dioxide; Daniel Rutherford discovered nitrogen. James Hutton's writings on the sources of rocks formed the basis for modern geology.

The technological developments of the Scottish Enlightenment led directly to the emergence of the country as a modern industrial power. The traditional craft of weaving was mechanized: James Watt's steam-engine-powered looms turned out massive amounts of quality woolens and linens for export. The rich iron and coal fields of the Central Lowlands yielded up the raw materials that soon had blast furnaces glowing and factory wheels turning. Glasgow was the leader in heavy industry and by 1840 was the shipbuilding center of the world.

URBAN DECAY

While middle-class Scots found new prosperity and a few grew rich, the Industrial Revolution in Scotland resulted in some of the worst living conditions in Europe. The poor and displaced people of the Highlands flocked to the mines and factories, often crowding together in squalid, crime-ridden slums. Before reform legislation was passed in the mid-1800s, women and children were victimized by employers, with girls as young as six hauling hundred-pound sacks of coal fourteen hours a day.

The streets of Edinburgh about 1840. Living conditions were deplorable for Scotland's poor urban residents during the Industrial Revolution.

The appalling living conditions in industrial Scotland led to political developments that were to mark the country from then until the present. The two chief political parties in Great Britain in the 1800s were the Conservatives, who stood for the interest of the wealthy landowners and industrialists, and the more democratic, reform-minded Liberals. Both, however, were parties of gentlemen in which the working classes had little part. To give the workers a voice, James Kier Hardie, head of the Scottish Miners' Federation, founded the Scottish Labour Party in 1888. Hardie was elected to Parliament where he and fellow party members merged with left-wing Liberals to form the British Labour Party in 1908. Hardie's successor, Ramsay MacDonald, became in 1924 the first Labour member and the first Scot to become prime minister of Great Britain.

HOME RULE

Many events and trends of the twentieth century—migration across the border in both directions, the expanding economies, the world wars in which English and Scots fought and died together—acted to strengthen the ties between the two countries. The differences between them were fast disappearing. But a sizeable segment of the population had never given up the idea of home rule—that Scots should run the affairs of Scotland without interference from London.

When the Labour Party dropped home rule as a priority in 1958, the Scottish National Party moved into the vacuum, campaigning for full independence and electing members to Parliament at Labour's expense. A national referendum on devolution—the surrendering by London of certain powers to a Scottish Parliament—failed in 1979, and the independence movement was then squelched by the Conservative governments of Margaret Thatcher and John Major. It flared anew when Labour won a majority in 1997, promising a new referendum. On September 11, 1997, the Scots voted by a three to one majority to restore the Parliament that had been dissolved in 1707.

The circle was now almost complete. In the span of seven hundred years, Scotland had gone from an independent nation with its own sovereign, to a nation sharing a ruler with England, to a union with England, and now was moving back toward full independence. It remained to be seen exactly what form devolution would take or whether a new century would see a complete break with England.

Scotland Today

5

Almost three centuries after uniting with England, Scotland was still struggling to establish its identity. As one writer, James Meek, put it, "Scotland may be less than a nation-state, but it is far more than a state of mind."[13] While many people predicted that the inundation of English culture—particularly the mass media—would snuff out traditional Scottish institutions, a Scottish flavor still permeates social and political institutions.

Either deliberately or instinctively, the Scots have taken paths separate from those of their larger neighbor. Many Scottish traditions—even the Scots language—might well have been discarded had they not been vehicles for defining the Scots as separate from the English. As a result of the Scots' desire for an identity, the culture and social structure of the country is distinctively Scottish.

Government

Nowhere is the struggle for identity more pronounced than in the Scots' quest for self-government. In 1999 they regained their own Parliament, but it seemed that no one, neither in Scotland nor in England, knew exactly what the Scottish Parliament was supposed to do. In the process of "devolution," responsibilities were supposed to be transferred from London to Edinburgh. Which responsibilities? No one was quite sure, but the Scots and the English were confident the uncertainty would somehow work itself out.

Meanwhile, Scotland still sent members to the Parliament in London, which was to retain responsibility for national defense, foreign policy, and other matters affecting the entire United Kingdom. The Scottish Parliament was to have control of local matters, such as education and agriculture. But what about all the matters in between those that were clearly national or clearly local, such as agricultural subsidies or welfare payments? It was evident that devolution was to be a process of evolution.

Having finally regained their own Parliament after almost three hundred years, the Scots (in typical fashion) can find little

65

Edinburgh's Holyrood Palace, the traditional residence of Scottish royalty. The building for the newly formed Scottish Parliament will be constructed near the palace.

good to say about it. While no one knows exactly what Parliament is *supposed* to do, one thing it has managed to do is spend money, something many electorates might object to but guaranteed to generate grumbling among the Scots. They grumbled about the cost of the new Parliament building under construction near Holyrood Palace in Edinburgh. They even grumbled when the MSPs (Members of Scottish Parliament) voted commemorative medallions for themselves at a cost of fifty-six pounds, about eighty-five U.S. dollars each.

While the national government tries to sort itself out, local government is highly organized and highly efficient. In 1975 the cumbersome system of dozens of city, burgh, and county governments was reorganized. The number of local governments was cut by more than half and the country divided into nine regions: Borders, Central, Dumfries and Galloway, Fife, Grampian, Highland, Lothian, Strathclyde, and Tayside; with separate regions for the Western Isles, Orkney Islands, and Shetland Islands. The regions are subdivided into fifty-three districts, including individual districts for the cities of Edinburgh, Glasgow, Dundee, and Aberdeen.

Local governments are run by regional and district councils to which representatives are elected every four years. The work of the councils is financed by a combination of funds from the central government of the United Kingdom and from a poll tax levied on every adult. The regional councils and the district councils within each region plan for the delivery of services. Education, police and fire protection, transportation, and social work are regional responsibilities, while districts monitor housing, sanitation, libraries, and recreation.

THE ECONOMY

In the nineteenth century Scotland progressed more rapidly than any nation in Europe from an agricultural economy to one dominated by heavy industry. That shift benefited Scotland so greatly that in the twentieth century the country clung too long to its standbys of shipbuilding, engineering,

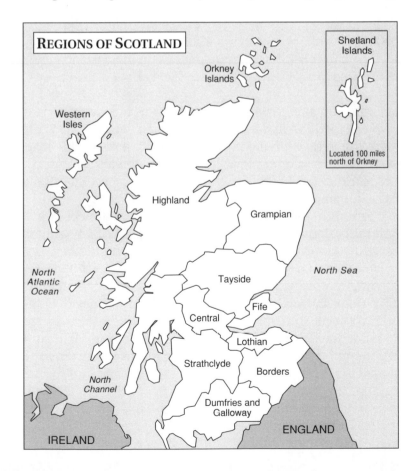

MISSED OPPORTUNITY

When vast oil and gas deposits were discovered under the North Sea in 1969, Scotland expected it to turn into an economic bonanza. While the oil industry has provided considerable employment opportunities, Scottish industry failed to take full advantage of the discovery and establish home-based companies to serve the new market.

In his study of the Scottish oil industry, William Pike described this missed opportunity, as quoted in *Scotland in the 20th Century*, edited by T. M. Devine and R. J. Finlay:

> Scottish industry simply did not understand the oil and gas industry or its requirements until the opportunity presented by the North Sea had already been lost and foreign companies were firmly entrenched. . . . Nor can the oil and gas companies be faulted for utilising their traditional infrastructure to exploit the discoveries in the North Sea. In the volatile international market, they simply could not afford the luxury of waiting for a suitable infrastructure to develop in Scotland.

mining, and steel. When those industries fell victim to foreign competition in the second half of the century, the Scots were late in diversifying their economy. As a result the Scottish economy is not as healthy as that of the rest of Europe. There are areas of prosperity, but they face uncertain futures in a changing global economic picture.

Agriculture remains an important part of the economy, primarily the raising of cattle and sheep. Scottish wool is renowned for its high quality, and the area around Aberdeen is famous for its beef. The Scottish beef industry is just now starting to recover from the "mad cow" disease scare of the mid-1990s, however. Export of British beef was severely restricted for a time after some cattle—mostly dairy—were found to have a disease that posed a threat to human health if consumed. Forestry is also increasing in importance as massive pinetree plantations have been created, but for the most part agriculture in Scotland has been adequate enough only to fill Scotland's needs.

The heavy industries that moved Scotland into the modern world—shipbuilding, iron, coal, and steel—were sustained through the first half of the twentieth century by the two world wars. After World War II, when much of Europe (including England) moved toward "lighter" industries such as automobile manufacturing and other consumer goods, Scotland (aided by government subsidies) propped up its outmoded mines and shipyards, which global competition was rapidly rendering obsolete.

Faced with rapid erosion of its economic base in the 1960s and 1970s, the country established the Scottish Development Agency in 1975 to encourage new industries. The Agency succeeded in attracting several electronics and computer firms, and most of the growth of employment in the last quarter of the century was in the "Silicon Glen" area of the Central Lowlands.

CONCERNS

Two worrisome aspects, however, face the Scottish electronics industry. First, the electronics industry in Scotland is heavily slanted toward the manufacturing of hardware, with little development of software and new products. Second, Scotland's relatively late entry into the computer field has meant that most of the companies—more than 80 percent— have been branches of foreign companies or owned by multinational corporations. As a result, according to economist Ivan Turok, "the prospects for self-sustaining, internally generated growth of the Scottish electronics industry cannot yet be described as promising."[14]

Oil and gas production is another Scottish industry that has been less promising than was hoped. The discovery of large deposits of oil under the floor of the North Sea in 1969 was hailed as the start of an economic boom. Two factors made the anticipated boom only a modest swell. The oil revenues went to the entire United Kingdom, not just Scotland, much to the chagrin of the Scots. The companies involved in the exploration and

Oil-industry tugboats in the harbor at Aberdeen, a major service center for North Sea petroleum.

production are mostly foreign. Thus, while the northeast part of the country has seen considerable oil-related employment, the crash of the industry in 1985 and the resulting loss of jobs showed Scotland the inherent insecurity of an oil-based economy.

Scotland's failure to gain a secure foothold in the electronics and oil industries has forced it to rely more on what it traditionally has done well. Banking and finance are strong, just as they were in the 1800s. Textiles and woolens are major exports. Tourism is a major source of income and employment, with the number of foreign visitors rising from 1.4 million in 1987 to 2.1 million in 1997. And of course, the Scots remain, as always, unequalled in the distilling of whisky.

Sheep shearing on the Isle of Skye, the largest of the Inner Hebrides. Scotland is well known for its fine woolens.

THE CHANGING POPULATION

Changes in the Scottish economy have resulted in changes in the population. Unemployment was 6.4 percent of the workforce in 1997, according to the Government Statistical Service, higher than in the United Kingdom as a whole but much improved from 9.3 percent in 1994. Other figures, however, indicate that the improvement may be owing to the fact that many people who cannot find work leave the country. The Government Records Office (GRO) estimated that about two thousand more people moved out of Scotland than moved into the country in 1998.

Most of the people leaving Scotland tend to be young, a circumstance reflected in demographics that indicate an aging population. Between 1991 and 1998 the percentage of the population under thirty years of age dropped by 14 percent, according to GRO figures. At the same time the percentage of persons more than sixty years old increased 5 percent. Over the next twenty years these percentages are expected to drop 35 percent and increase 55 percent, respectively.

The combination of emigration and aging raises the likelihood that Scotland is headed for a population decrease. The GRO forecasts that by 2021 the number of people in Scotland will fall below 5 million for the first time in half a century.

STANDARD OF LIVING

Even though many of its people emigrate, Scotland enjoys one of the highest standards of living in Europe. Although the Scots earn 8 percent less on the average than their fellow citizens of the United Kingdom, prices are even lower. The average home in Scotland, for instance, costs more than 18 percent less than in the U.K. as a whole.

As the price of housing comes increasingly within reach of the average Scot, more are becoming home owners rather than renters. Thanks to an aggressive program by the government-backed National Housing Agency, which works with builders and lenders, more than 60 percent of Scottish dwellings were occupied by the owners in 1997 as compared to only 44 percent in 1987.

The combination of higher home ownership and lower unemployment seems to have brought a certain stability to Scottish society. Slightly more than 8,800 crimes were reported per hundred-thousand population in 1996, 10 percent less than in

STEALING THE SHOW

When the Scottish Parliament reconvened on July 1, 1999, for the first time since 1707, the star of the show was not First Minister Donald Dewar or even Her Majesty Queen Elizabeth II. Instead, the media spotlight was on actor Sean Connery, an active member of the Scottish National Party and an outspoken supporter of complete independence for Scotland.

Connery did not have any official role in the ceremonies. He was not among the many speakers, but chose to make his personal statement by wearing full Highland dress—kilt and all—instead of the business suits that had been decreed by the government.

"It's a pity that the national dress is not being celebrated," he was quoted in a story in *The Times* of London the next day. "There is a Scottish Parliament tartan after all. Most politicians tend to ignore Highland dress, which is sad."

Lisa Stewart of Edinburgh, one of the many onlookers, agreed, telling *Times* reporter Gillian Harris, "If Sean Connery can make the effort, so can the politicians. It is an important part of being Scottish and this is such an important day."

England. This figure represented a steep decline from the approximately 9,800 crimes per hundred-thousand population in 1994. One area in which crime fell was drunk driving, which declined 6 percent from 1997 to 1998, indicating a corresponding drop in alcoholism, long a severe problem in urban areas.

On the other hand, drug use has increased. *The Scottish Express* reported in 1998 that Scotland "has one of Europe's worst drug abuse records with around eight thousand people using heroin in Glasgow alone."[15] Also on the rise is acquired immune deficiency syndrome (AIDS). The number of reported AIDS cases rose 8 percent in 1997, although the frequency of the disease is far less common than in the rest of the U.K.

EDUCATION

One reason that the overall crime rate is down in Scotland may be that more people are taking advantage of the educational system. Although the population has remained constant, enrollment in public schools rose 2 percent between 1986 and 1996 while the number of students in higher education almost doubled.

Perhaps nowhere else in the world is education valued as strongly as in Scotland. It is an article of faith that clever lads and lassies, however humble their origins, can succeed by hard study and hard work. Although critics have challenged traditional forms of education as emphasizing conformity and stifling initiative, Scots continue to put their trust in public education. Private schools enroll a far smaller percentage of students than do their counterparts in England.

Ever since John Knox preached that education—education for all—was central to religious freedom, schools and the Kirk were an important part of the fabric of Scottish life. Although control of education by the Kirk was removed in 1929 and now rests with regional councils, the influence of generations of church-run schools continues to be felt. Scottish schools are highly traditional in curricula and teaching methods, and the basic mission has remained one of preparing students for the workplace.

EDUCATION REFORMS

Reformers have made some inroads. The old system of assigning students to either academic or vocational secondary schools based on tests given at age twelve was abandoned in 1965. The age at which students may leave school was raised to sixteen in 1973. Efforts to make secondary education beyond that age totally open to all students have been unsuccessful. While all students may continue in the "Higher Grades," their performance on tests determines how many advanced courses they may take. Only those advancing to the more challenging and academic courses have a reasonable expectation of entering colleges or universities.

Still, the percentage of students continuing their education is high. As of 1993, 38 percent of Scottish students entered colleges or universities compared to about 10 percent in England.

Tourists visit St. Salvator's College, part of Saint Andrew's University in Fife. Founded in 1411, Saint Andrew's is the oldest university in Scotland.

THE ROLE OF THE CHURCH

The impact of the Presbyterian Church in Scotland has gone far beyond spiritual matters. From the time of John Knox onward, the Kirk has been at the center of social and political developments. The role of the church in bringing about personal freedom for the Scottish people is described by Alexander Martin, moderator of the United Free Church, as quoted in *Scotland in the 20th Century*, edited by T. M. Devine and R. J. Finlay:

> No one who knew their Scottish history would deny that the Church had fulfilled many a notable public service in the past. It has been on the floor of the General Assemblies [of the Kirk] rather than in the corrupt estates [Parliament] or Privy Council [the monarch's advisers] that the battle of the Scottish people for freedom had been fought and won. The burden of the poor was borne for centuries by the Church unaided and in her system of education she laid during the past ages the foundation of a democracy in which all barriers were down, and the way was open and free for all.

Higher education has a long history in Scotland, with the first university, Saint Andrew's, founded in 1411. Glasgow and Aberdeen came shortly afterward, and Edinburgh University got its start in 1583. In the 1960s the four ancient institutions were joined by the universities of Strathclyde in Glasgow, of Heriot-Watt in Edinburgh, of Stirling, and of Dundee, the first two having been upgraded from technical schools.

A typical university education begins with two years of general study, after which students may stay two more years to complete an "Honours" degree in a specific area of study or do one additional year of general studies for an "Ordinary" degree. As in the rest of the United Kingdom, universities are entirely funded by the government and students pay no tuition or fees.

RELIGION

Although education is no longer primarily a function of the church, religion still plays a major role in the life of Scotland. While John Knox's Kirk never fulfilled its founder's dream of controlling every aspect of culture and government, it nevertheless dominated Scottish life for centuries. As historian Graham Walker wrote, "Presbyterianism was central to a moral outlook which galvanized Scots to meet the challenges of empire building, missionary work, wealth creation and governance."[16] Religion's influence has waned in the twentieth century but still remains an underlying factor in Scottish society.

With the alliance of the two main branches of Presbyterianism—the Church of Scotland and the Free Church—in 1929, active membership numbered 1.3 million, 27 percent of the population and twice the number of Roman Catholics. Membership has declined from the 1960s and at the end of the century stood at about 15 percent.

The Presbyterian Church is far more liberal than in Knox's day or even a few decades ago, taking a strong stand against nuclear weapons and taking a more active role in relieving the plight of the urban poor. In a move that would have outraged Knox, whose opinion of women was decidedly poor, the Kirk began ordaining female ministers in the 1960s.

Crossmichael Kirk in the village of Crossmichael. The Kirk, or Presbyterian Church, is the main religious denomination in Scotland.

A "FINE HEALTHFUL GAME"

Although most authorities credit the Scots with the invention of golf, the Dutch claim that it derived from a much older sport, *kolven*, that originated in the Netherlands. While *kolven* involved sending a ball toward a target by striking it with a stick, the Scots were the first to make hitting the ball into a hole the object of the game.

For centuries golf was confined mainly to Scotland. As late as 1830 a writer from England felt it necessary to give his readers this description of the game, included in *Sporting Scotland* by John Burnett:

> The old Scots game of golf is a gigantic variety of billiards; the table being a certain space of green, sometimes of many hundreds of yards in extent—the holes situated here and there at great distances; and the balls, which are very hard, stuffed with feathers, being swung to and fro by means of long queues [sticks] with elastic shafts—a fine healthful game.

> The first national tournament, the Open Championship (known in the United States as the British Open), was conducted in 1860 and was won by a Scot every year until 1888. It would not be until 1921 that Bobby Jones would become the first American to win the Open.

The Presbyterian Church, while dominant, is not the only major Protestant denomination. The Scottish Episcopal Church is widespread and is especially strong in the northeast. In the far west, remnants of the fundamentalist Kirk—the "Wee Frees"—remain and those areas virtually shut down on Sundays.

At the same time, Roman Catholicism has been on the rise, primarily as a result of immigration from the Catholics of Northern Ireland, who have come to Scotland seeking jobs and fleeing the religious violence in their homeland. Some estimates at the end of the century placed the number of Catholics at about eight hundred thousand, approximately the same as for the Church of Scotland.

LITERATURE AND THE ARTS

With the Kirk frowning on what it considered frivolous endeavors, classical music and dance never had much of a chance in Scotland. Likewise, sculpture and painting (other than portraiture) never developed as fully as in the rest of Europe. Thanks, however, to a heritage of storytelling and a national emphasis on education, Scotland has produced a body of literature far out of proportion to its size and population.

While Walter Scott made Scottish themes popular worldwide in the early 1800s, it was the language and earthy subject matter of Robert Burns that most influenced Scotland's outstanding writers of the twentieth century. His use of Scots helped keep the language alive as a vehicle for literature to be picked up after World War I by poet Hugh MacDairmid, who used colorful, long-forgotten words found only in Scots dictionaries. MacDairmid's themes, like those of Burns, celebrated the common people. Likewise novelist James Leslie Mitchell, who wrote under the name Lewis Grassic Gibbon, liberally flavored his English prose with Scots.

MacDairmid and Mitchell were the key figures in what was called the Scottish Renaissance of the 1920s and 1930s. Their chief disciples at the end of the century included novelists Alasdair Gray, James Kelman, and William McInvanny and poet Tom Leonard.

The doors of Glasgow's Willow Tea Room, built in 1903–1904 by Scottish architect Charles Rennie Mackintosh.

Drama has not fared as well in Scotland as has prose and poetry. The country has produced only one playwright of note, James Barrie, author of *Peter Pan.* Even so, Scotland annually hosts two of the most prestigious arts festivals in Europe—the Edinburgh International Festival and Glasgow's Mayfest—that feature not only plays, but also music and visual art.

Scotland has produced few painters of international fame. The portraits of Allan Ramsay in the 1700s and Henry Raeburn in the 1800s are the most famous works, along with the breathtaking Highland landscapes of Horatio McCullough.

In architecture Scotland has strayed little from traditional styles except in Glasgow, which features some of the most striking modern buildings in Europe. Glasgow architecture has been heavily influenced

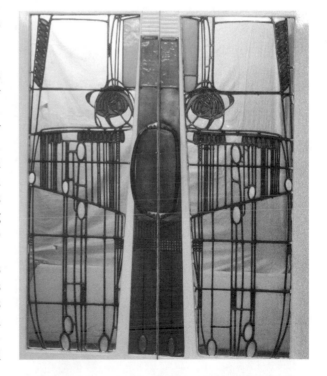

by Charles Rennie Mackintosh (1868–1928), a noted interior designer whose work during his lifetime was admired mostly outside Scotland. Elsewhere most new buildings are either simple and utilitarian or follow the Italian classical tradition popularized by Scottish architect Robert Adam (1728–1792).

Since the United Kingdom became a part of the European Economic Community in 1973, Scotland has moved rapidly into the modern world. Some Scots worry that the movement is too rapid—that Scottish identity will dissolve as the nations of Europe grow closer in culture and economy. They seek to avoid such a fate by turning time and again to their past. As Scotland builds a society for the new millennium, it is making sure that the new structure is firmly founded on centuries of tradition.

POPULAR CULTURE

6

Just as they have developed a social and governmental structure distinct from that of England, the Scots have relied heavily on tradition to fashion a popular culture all their own. Ask a native of England what tatties and neeps are and you would probably get a blank look in return. Likewise for a philabeg, a sporran, a pibroch, or a caber. A Scot, however, and especially a Highlander, should savor those words. After all, they are descriptive of the traditional aspects that perhaps best define the popular image of Scotland.

HAGGIS

To Robert Burns, it may have been "a glorious sight, warm-reekin [smelling], rich,"[17] but it's safe to say that haggis is decidedly less appealing to most people outside Scotland and a good

Haggis is presented to diners during a Burns Supper. Robert Burns's "Address to a Haggis" is usually recited as the traditional dish is presented and served. 79

many people in it. While it may be the national dish, it is one that takes some getting used to and not one for finicky eaters.

Haggis (the word comes from the French *hachis*, meaning finely chopped) is a pudding in the old, British sense of a meat dish encrusted with suet, or fat, and boiled in a bag. Although now served in the finest restaurants, it was originally a dish for the poor, determined to use every part of a sheep except the "baa."

Haggis is made by taking a sheep's pluck (heart, liver, windpipe) and lights (lungs), chopping them together with beef suet, and allowing the mixture to soak overnight. Oatmeal, onions, seasonings, and gravy are stirred in; the resulting mixture is stuffed into a tightly sealed bag—traditionally a sheep's stomach—and boiled for several hours. Haggis is served hot and almost always accompanied by *clapshott*, a mixture of tatties and neeps (potatoes and turnips to non-Scots).

Haggis is served year-round in restaurants, although Robert Burns would hardly recognize some of the fancier varieties found in "nouveau Scottish" establishments. The dish comes into its own, however, every January 25 when Burns Suppers are held all over the country to celebrate the poet's birthday. The highlight of the evening comes when the haggis is borne with great pomp into the room as Burns's "Address to a Haggis" is recited. At the proper moment in the reading—

An cut you up with ready slight [skill],
Trenching your gushing entrails bright . . .[18]

—the pudding is sliced open and served.

Many Scots probably eat haggis only at Burns Suppers and only then because they consider it a patriotic duty. Highly spiced, brimming with fat, and having an extremely strong taste, it is not a dish for the sensitive stomach.

WHISKY

The haggis at Burns Suppers is washed down with copious amounts of another Scottish tradition—whisky. In the fourteenth century, Scottish monks began making a strong alcoholic drink from barley. They called it *uisge bretha*, or "water of life," later anglicized to whisky. Eventually whisky distilling grew from small enterprises—some of them illegal stills hidden deep in glens—to a major industry, and whisky became Scotland's national drink.

BURNS'S "ADDRESS TO A HAGGIS"

While Robert Burns's best-known poem is doubtless "Auld Lang Syne," his "Address to a Haggis" has a special place in the hearts of Scots as it lauds their national dish, equating it with the hardiness of the people and dismissing other fare as inferior and unworthy. This excerpt, taken from a version found on the Internet site www.rabbie-burns.com, is an outstanding example of Burns's humor and also a good example of the Scots language:

Fair fa' your honest, sonsie [cheerful] face,
Great chieftain o the puddin'-race!
Aboon them a' ye tak your place,
Painch, tripe, or thairm [guts]:
Weel are ye wordy of a grace
As lang's as my arm. . . .

Is there that owre [over] his French ragout [stew],
Or olio [mixture] that wad staw [sicken] a sow,
Or fricassee wad mak her spew
Wi perfect sconner [disgust],
Looks down wi sneering, scornfu view
On sic a dinner?

Poor Devil! See him owre his trash,
As feckless [weak] as a wither'd rash [reed],
His spindle shank [skinny leg] a guid whip-lash,
His nieve [fist] a nit [nut]:
Thro bloody flood or field to dash,
O how unfit!

But mark the Rustic, haggis-fed,
The trembling earth resounds his tread,
Clap [held] in his walie [choice] nieve a blade,
He'll make it whissle;
An legs and arms, an head will sned [cut off],
Like taps [tops] o thrissle [thistles].

For reasons unknown the spirits made in Scotland are called "Scotch" instead of "Scottish" and the word *whisky* is never spelled "whiskey," as elsewhere. The term Scotch whisky is never heard in Scotland, except from tourists, since it is assumed that whisky automatically means that which is

Barrels of Scotch, the famous whisky Scotland has been producing for over six hundred years.

produced in Scotland. Indeed, whisky that is exported cannot be labeled "Scotch" unless it is distilled and bottled entirely within the country's borders.

The finest whiskies are "single malt," meaning that they are produced only by a single distillery. Single malts have distinct tastes, usually imparted by the water used. At the Talisker distillery on the Isle of Skye, for instance, the spring water filters through peat, which gives the whisky a sharp, smoky taste. Connoisseurs can readily identify brands of single malt whiskey in the same way experts can identify fine wines.

Since single malts are expensive and time-consuming to produce, a shortcut was devised whereby colorless alcohol from several distilleries is mixed with whisky made from lighter grains and cereals and sometimes with water and food coloring. The results are "blended" whiskies that account for 95 percent of all Scotch whisky sold.

The true Scot would never dream of putting ice in single malt whisky, much less mixing it with anything like soda. It is meant to be sipped slowly and savored, no matter what the time of day or night. As Walter Scott wrote, "It is the only liquor fit for a gentleman to drink in the morning if he can have the good fortune to come by it . . . or after dinner either."[19]

HIGHLAND DRESS

Most, if not all, of the revelers at a Burns Supper will be sporting another distinctively Scottish item. Highland dress, once considered crude and barbaric—and outlawed as subversive from 1746 to 1782—has made quite a comeback. Within a few generations of its banishment, it was being worn proudly by British royalty. Today, it pops up on street corners in Highland towns and is a popular trend for formal weddings throughout Scotland.

The terminology of Highland dress can be confusing. A tartan can refer either to a garment or the striped and checkered patterns woven into it. Plaid (pronounced "played" by the true Highlander) likewise can be a pattern or the clothing itself.

THE NOSE KNOWS

When young, pre-aging single malt whiskies are combined with other ingredients to make the popular and less expensive blended whiskies, master blenders test each batch to see if the mixture is just right. Unlike the wine connoisseur, however, who may swirl the liquid in a glass, sniff it, and finally taste it, the whisky blender relies only on the nose.

Wine tasters may use water to clear their palates between tests. Whisky, much higher in alcohol content, tends to anesthetize the taste buds rendering the blender unable to judge quality. An experienced blender, therefore, only sniffs a whisky to pronounce it fit to bottle. A master blender will be able to detect more than a hundred separate flavors and characters.

The blender uses a special glass, wide at the base and much narrower at the rim, in order to concentrate the aromas. Water is added to release the esters and aldehydes and thus make the aromas stronger. Distillers are careful to use only clear spring water with a low mineral content.

Taste, however, is important, and experts John Lamond and Robin Tucek have developed a scale by which they rate various whiskies. Scores are given from 1 to 10 on sweetness and on the peatiness, or the smokiness of the flavor. Lamond and Tucek have added a third scale on availability since some whiskies are no longer made or are made in such small quantities as to be hard to find.

Highland dress evolved from the multipurpose garment called either the *feileadh mor* (great plaid) or *breacan feile* (belted plaid). Part of this long piece of wool was wound around the waist and then belted. The remainder was worn over the shoulder and held in place with a brooch. The upper part could be used as a cloak in bad weather, and the clansman unlucky enough to be caught outside after dark could wrap himself up in it and use it as a sleeping bag.

From the great plaid developed the *feile beag*, or phil-abeg, the kilt that forms the basic modern Highland dress. Worn only by men, they are made from pieces of woolen cloth up to twenty-seven feet long folded into numerous pleats. The finest kilts are entirely hand sewn and can cost upwards of four hundred dollars, four times the cost of a machine-made kilt.

Scottish men in kilts and sporrans. The man at far left also wears a sgian dhu *in his right stocking.*

The formal Highland dress is completed by black shoes with silver buckles, tall woolen stockings, and a black velvet jacket over a dress shirt with a frilly front. A dirk, or dagger, is worn at the side, with a smaller weapon, the *sgian dhu*, or black knife, tucked in the top of the right stocking. A sporran,

or leather purse, once purely functional but now highly decorated, hangs in front of the kilt. Topping the costume is a bonnet, sometimes adorned with an eagle feather.

Tartan Patterns

The tartan patterns in kilts, known as "setts," originally were wholly decorative and had nothing to do with individual clans. Instead the tartans varied by region and by individual weaver depending on what natural substances were available to make colors. Saint John's wort was used for yellow, elderberry for blue, broom for green, and sundew for purple.

It was not until after Walter Scott convinced King George IV to wear a kilt on a visit to Scotland in 1822 that specific tartans for families became popular. The popularity increased and the tartan industry came into its own when Queen Victoria began spending her summers in Scotland, and those in her court donned Highland dress.

Eventually each family had to have its own one-of-a-kind pattern. Members of one clan, finding that the pattern it chose was the same as a hereditary rival, made theirs different by, say, changing a white stripe to yellow, even going to the trouble of having generations of family portraits touched up. Today anyone, Scottish or not, can register a "clan" tartan by paying a fee of about sixty-five dollars. More than three thousand tartans are registered.

Folk Music

Another staple of the Burns Suppers is music, Scottish style. Scotland has no tradition of classical European music, but even the disapproval of the Kirk could not altogether banish the legendary Celtic love of folk music. When that disapproval lost much of its force in the 1800s, traditional music enjoyed a resurgence that still continues. Burns was almost as influential in music as he was in literature, collecting, rewriting, and publishing volumes of songs. In modern times folk music gatherings, *ceilidh* in Gaelic, are as popular in Glasgow as they are in rural Highland towns, the chief instruments being the harp, fife, lute, accordion, and fiddle.

Bagpipes, the musical instrument most identified with Scotland, are not generally found in *ceilidh* bands. They are

Traditionally dressed pipers play as they march in formation. Pipe bands perform for both recreation and competition.

so loud as to drown out all the other instruments. They would definitely be used, however, to lead diners on a procession into a Burns Supper.

Bagpipe music is like haggis—an "acquired taste." One either relishes it or can hardly stand it. Almost no one is neutral when it comes to the piercing, discordant wail of the pipes. The sound of "Scotland the Brave" or "The Bonnie Banks of Loch Lomond" may bring a tear to the eye of a Scot, but it will lead many others to put their fingers in their ears.

The bagpipe was not invented in Scotland. Indeed, similar instruments have been used in several ancient civilizations around the world. Even so, it has come to be identified almost exclusively with Scotland and has become the national instrument.

The bagpipe operates on the same principle as a clarinet or oboe. The musician blows air across a reed, and the vibration of the reed creates sound. Different notes are sounded by the placement of fingers on finger holes. There, the similarity to most reed instruments ends.

Bagpipe reeds are not located on the mouthpiece, but inside the three "drone" pipes and in the "chanter." The drones produce only a single note: an A below the piano's low A for the two smaller, or "tenor" drones; and A an octave below that for the larger "bass" drone.

Pipers play their melodies on the chanter, against the background notes provided by the drones. Air blown through the mouthpiece, or "blowpipe," goes into a bag and from the bag through the drones and chanter. The trick in bagpipe playing is to keep the flow of air steady. When the player pauses for a breath, the bag is squeezed between the body and elbow to keep air going through the drones and chanter. Coordinating between blowing and squeezing takes considerable practice.

Unique Qualities

Bagpipes have peculiarities found in no other instruments. Since a steady flow of air passes over the reeds, a piper cannot play the same note twice in succession as a clarinet player would—by blowing twice. Instead the piper must separate like notes with a "grace note," a different intervening note played so quickly that the *impression* of what one hears is of the same note played twice.

Another bagpipe oddity is that the chanter is capable of playing only seven notes instead of the twelve notes found on the scale typically used in western music. As a result, many tunes cannot be played on bagpipes and the ones written especially for the bagpipe scale tend to sound very similar.

Not all bagpipes are alike. The *pìob mhór*, or Great Highland pipe, is the one most commonly pictured. Because it is so loud—it is impossible to play bagpipes softly—the Great Highland pipe is most often played outdoors. Smaller, "reel pipes" are used for indoor dancing, as are half-sized pipes.

Bagpipes are extremely popular in Scotland, and their popularity is growing worldwide. Most police departments and military units have pipe bands, and the pipe band is to many Scottish schools what the marching band is to American schools.

Leisure and Festivals

Scots enjoy themselves on many occasions. Their long-standing reputation as a morose people, fostered primarily by the English, is misleading. As their many festivals and gatherings demonstrate, the Scots have a healthy appetite for fun.

Special nights other than Burns's birthday call for special celebrations in Scotland. Halloween is a major holiday, with children going door-to-door performing songs or skits in exchange for treats and with adults gathering for parties. New Year's Eve, known in Scotland as "Hogmanay," is even more festive, with the traditional Scottish reserve vanishing in many kisses and toasts as the clock strikes midnight.

On a more regular basis the Scots, like their counterparts throughout Great Britain and Ireland, enjoy trips to the "local"—the public house, or pub—for a pint of beer or a dram of whisky. Perhaps as a lingering effect of the Kirk, however, pubs are far less common than in England or Ireland. Dining out has increased in popularity, thanks in large part to an influx of non-European restaurants in recent years. Still, the Scots' tastes tend toward fried, fatty foods, one reason they have one of the highest heart attack rates in Europe.

A pub in Aberdeen, Scotland. The pub is a popular place for Scots to relax and enjoy a beer or whisky.

SPORTS

If the Scots have an appetite for fun, they have an absolute passion for sports. Golf was invented in Scotland and remains the country's most popular participant sport. The first record

of golf dates from 1457 when King James II tried to outlaw the sport so that his subjects would practice archery instead. The first golf club was founded at Leith in 1744, and from Saint Andrew's, established ten years later, came the basic rules of the game. Unlike many other countries in which golf is primarily for the wealthy, Scotland provides golf for everyone with more than four hundred courses, most of them public.

For the more athletic, there is rugby football, somewhat similar to American football and played in Scotland by teams of amateurs. Also popular is shinty, a team game played with sticks and a ball, that resembles field hockey.

Association football, or soccer, is the primary spectator sport. Most larger cities and towns have professional teams that draw thousands of ardent fans. In Edinburgh and Glasgow football is literally close to being a religious experience. Both cities have two teams—one predominantly Protestant, the other Catholic—and many people defined others by the team they follow. Other sports attracting good crowds are rugby football and horse racing.

Soccer is the most popular spectator sport in Scotland. Most cities and towns have professional teams.

With so much of the Scottish landscape wild and undeveloped, it is also little wonder that outdoor sports attract huge followings. Fishing is enjoyed by people of all social classes, while hunting is primarily for the more affluent. Many hunters eagerly await each August 12, the "Glorious Twelfth," when red grouse shooting season begins; people have been known to use helicopters and even parachutes in contests to see who can get the first grouse from field to table.

HIGHLAND GAMES

Hundreds of years ago Highland clan chiefs held competitions among their warriors to see who was the strongest, swiftest, and most agile. From such military exercises evolved the Highland games, sometimes called "gatherings," in which hordes of natives and tourists descend on towns and villages and the sounds of bagpipes mingle with the grunts of large, straining, sweaty men.

The first thing one notices when arriving on the scene of a Highland gathering is the incessant skirling of bagpipes. As many as a dozen pipe bands participate, following one another in succession and occasionally playing all together as they march around the arena in a truly spectacular procession.

The gatherings, however, are more about muscle than music. The running and jumping events are those to be found at any track meet: hundred-yard run, mile run, long jump, high jump, along with local variations. The Braemar Gathering, for instance, is held at the foot of 2,800-foot Morrone Hill, to the summit of which runners must scramble in the traditional hill race. Another twist to the running events is that some traditionalists compete wearing kilts, putting them at a decided disadvantage against lighter-clad rivals.

While the runners are circling the arena, more activities are going on in the center. Scottish country dancing is a feature of every Highland games, with contestants—mostly young girls—competing in the Highland fling, hornpipe, Irish jig, and other traditional favorites. They are accompanied by a piper, whose music may be at odds with that of a pipe band only a few dozen yards away. Off in another corner the pipers have their own competition, playing marches, reels, and the classical bagpipe tunes known as *piobaireachd* in Gaelic, *pibroch* in Scots. Elsewhere in the arena, teams from armed service units compete in a tug-o-war.

THE "HEAVIES"

The stars of Highland games are the "heavies," brawny men who specialize in throwing heavy objects. The hammer and shot are present, as in most meets worldwide, but the Scots have in addition retained the "staine," or stone, that was used before being replaced by the shot when cannons were invented.

Another popular event is weight shifting, sometimes called "weight-over-the-bar." Competitors stand with their back to a horizontal bar suspended between two poles and with one hand grasp a short chain attached to a weight. The weights are in two sizes—twenty-eight and fifty-six pounds. The competitor swings the weight back and forth between his legs in preparation, then heaves it up and back, hoping to

A STICKY SITUATION

One of the most famous athletes to compete in Highland games was not a Scot, but an Englishman named Geoff Capes. Capes, who was from Lincoln, won the caber toss at Braemar for six consecutive years starting in 1981. His most memorable year was 1982, not because of what happened during the competition but of what happened afterward.

The Braemar Gathering is one of the very oldest games, supposedly dating from a time before the year 1100 when King Malcolm III called the clansmen to the braes (hills) of Mar to choose the strongest and most skilled. Braemar is still very much associated with royalty. Balmoral Castle, a summer residence of every British monarch since Queen Victoria, is only a few miles to the east, and the reigning king or queen is always the patron of the games.

Since the caber toss is the highlight of the games, the winner receives his trophy from the queen, should she be present. When Capes stepped forward to receive the trophy from Queen Elizabeth II in 1982, he had forgotten to wash from his hand the resin used to ensure a good grip on the caber. He shook hands with the queen and when he tried to pull his hand away, found it was firmly stuck to the queen's glove.

Elizabeth laughed heartily, as did everyone around her. Capes was thunderstruck with embarrassment for a moment, then joined in the laughter. He took away, not only the prized Murray Challenge Trophy, but also a souvenir— a very sticky, soiled royal glove.

Geoff Capes, shown here with shot put, won the caber toss in the Highland Games for six consecutive years.

clear the bar. After each round the bar is raised until only one successful contestant remains.

The most eagerly awaited event is the tossing of the caber —a large and heavy wooden pole. The origins of caber tossing

A Highland Games competitor walks forward, balancing the caber against his shoulder as he prepares to toss it up and over.

are vague, but some experts think it began with loggers tossing tree trunks into streams to be floated to sawmills.

To toss the caber the athlete first balances it upright on the ground, then—keeping it balanced with a shoulder—slides his hands down carefully to the base. He lifts the caber, a feat in itself, and uses a shoulder to keep it upright.

When ready, the contestant trots forward, allowing the caber to begin to tilt forward. When he thinks the ideal moment has arrived, he heaves upward, flipping (hopefully) the caber into the air. The height of the toss doesn't matter; neither does the distance. The object of the toss is for the caber to flip over onto the end opposite from the one grasped by the athlete and then fall forward. The perfect toss, a "twelve o'clock," will see the caber flip over and fall forward directly away from the athlete. Points are deducted if it falls off to one side.

Cabers do not come in any standard length or weight. At Braemar contestants must place in preliminary rounds using lighter cabers before advancing to the finals. Then, and only then, are they allowed to try their luck with the famous Braemar Caber, measuring nineteen and three-quarters feet and weighing 132 pounds.

Contestants in almost every event, even the young dancers, can win prize money, and some of the athletes are professionals for whom Highland games are a second career. The prizes range from twelve pounds (eighteen dollars) in the children's sack race to three hundred pounds (four hundred and fifty dollars) for the winner of the Braemar Caber toss.

The elements that epitomize Scottish popular culture are by no means confined to Scotland. Generations of emigrants have either taken their heritage with them to new lands or have rediscovered it. Festivals featuring Highland games are conducted throughout the English-speaking world. Pipe bands have been formed everywhere from Houston to Honolulu. Many a military-style funeral will feature a piper, in full Highland dress, playing "Amazing Grace." Scotch whisky is consumed worldwide, although haggis—perhaps thankfully—is seldom found outside Scotland. Someone once called Scotland a state of mind rather than a state, and that state of mind knows no borders.

EPILOGUE

REBIRTH OF A NATION

Speaking at the opening of Scotland's new Parliament in 1999, Queen Elizabeth II said, "My prayers are with you all as you embark on this new and historic journey. I have trust in the good judgment of the Scottish people . . . I am confident in the future of Scotland."[20] A journey had indeed begun, but there was no certainty as to where it would lead.

Scotland had its own Parliament for the first time in almost three centuries, but no one knew exactly what it would have the power to do. Scotland had taken a step, but no one knew how large a step or if it would be the final step. Would Scotland remain a semi-autonomous state within the larger framework of Great Britain or would it go further and seek complete separation and independence?

Alex Salmond, leader of the Scottish National Party, was certain it would be the latter. "For many of us this is not the end of Scotland's journey. We aspire to return Scotland to the international community on the basis of equality among nations," he said at Parliament's opening.[21]

Scotland's new Parliament (pictured) convened in 1999. Scotland had not had its own Parliament since 1707.

REALITIES OF INDEPENDENCE

There is, indeed, much sentiment in Scotland to become independent of Great Britain, but some harsh realities lie underneath the layers of patriotic fervor. Scotland in 1999 received 32 percent more per capita of public spending than any other part of the United Kingdom: money for education, housing, health care. Where, critics of separation ask, would Scotland obtain these funds if independence were achieved?

Some observers also fear that Scottish desire for independence, if not realized, would cause it to become a festering sore in Britain, much like Quebec is to Canada. "This would be a tragedy of considerable proportions," wrote Peter Hennessy, professor of modern history at the University of London, "for it would waste precious years in which an acrimonious separation would divert the energies of England and Scotland."[22]

Most people seemed to doubt that such a bitter confrontation would develop. It seemed unlikely that the Scots, an intensely practical people, would allow the spirit of nationalism to override the economic advantages of remaining part of Britain while retaining a national identity. Indeed, First Minister Donald Dewar said that the new Parliament "revitalizes our place in the United Kingdom. This is about more than our politics and laws. This is about who we are."[23]

TAKING THEIR TIME

The people of the British Isles have a history of allowing things to work themselves out. Unlike the United States, the United Kingdom does not have a written constitution. Its citizens tend to let matters settle into a pattern rather than try to have everything spelled out in advance. No one in Scotland has seemed perturbed that the devolution of powers to the new Parliament might take awhile. Scottish cartoonist Ewen Bain once pictured a father talking to his son about devolution and evolution, the father saying, "No, son, they're not the same thing. Devolution takes longer."[24]

If Scotland was facing an uncertain future it was, after all, hardly the first time. The Scots would face a new Parliament, devolution, and the prospect of independence with a stoic

outlook born of centuries of adversity. Being a Scot has never been easy, but the Scots will never surrender their heritage or their pride. In the words of one of their greatest writers, Robert Louis Stevenson:

A Scottish man at work at the harbor in Mallaig, on the west coast of the Highlands region.

> The happiest lot on earth is to be born a Scotsman. You must pay for it in many ways, as for all other advantages on earth. . . . But somehow life is warmer and closer; the hearth burns more redly; the lights of home shine softer on the rainy street; the very names, endeared in verse and music, cling nearer around our hearts.[25]

FACTS ABOUT SCOTLAND

GEOGRAPHY

Land Area: 30,142 square miles (includes 787 islands).

Highest Point: Ben Nevis (4,406 feet).

Lowest Point: Sea level.

Highest Mountains: Ben Nevis (4,406 feet), Ben Macdhui (4,296 feet), Braeriach (4,252 feet), Cairntoul (4,241 feet), Cairngorm (4,084 feet), Ben Lawers (3,984 feet).

Major Rivers, Length: Tay (117 miles), Spey (110 miles), Clyde (106 miles), Tweed (96 miles), Dee (96 miles), Don (82 miles), Forth (66 miles).

Largest Lakes: Loch Lomond (area, 27 square miles; mean depth, 121 feet; maximum depth, 623 feet), Loch Ness (21.8 square miles; mean depth, 433 feet; maximum depth, 754 feet), Loch Awe (14.8 square miles; mean depth, 105 feet; maximum depth, 307 feet).

CLIMATE

	Avg. Rain	Avg. High(F)	Avg. Low(F)
Nairn (North)	24 inches	54 degrees	41 degrees
Oban (West)	58 inches	54 degrees	43 degrees
Edinburgh (Central)	27 inches	54 degrees	43 degrees
Dumfries (Lowlands)	41 inches	54 degrees	41 degrees

POPULATION

Estimated population in 1998: 5,120,000.

Population per Square Mile: 169.

Major Cities: Glasgow, 619,680; Edinburgh, 450,180; Aberdeen, 213,070; Dundee, 146,690.

Major Religious Groups: Church of Scotland (Presbyterian), 15 percent of population; Roman Catholic, 14 percent; Scottish Episcopal, 1 percent; other Christian, 1.5 percent; Muslim, 0.5 percent; Jewish, 0.5 percent.

Adult Literacy: 99 percent.

Life Expectancy: Women, 75.5 years; men 69.3 years.

ECONOMY

Major Industries: Agriculture, heavy machinery, electronics, distilling, oil and gas exploration equipment.

Chief Crops (1997): Barley, 1.8 million tons; potatoes, 1.1 million tons; wheat, 821,000 tons; oats, 121,000 tons.

Livestock Production (1997): Sheep, 9.5 million; cattle, 2.1 million; swine, 645,000.

Average Weekly Earnings: £272.4 ($435 U.S. dollars).

Unemployment Rate: 6.4 percent (1997).

NOTES

CHAPTER 2: THE PEOPLE

1. Quoted in James Meek, *The Land and People of Scotland*, Portraits of the Nations series. New York: J. B. Lippincott, 1990, p. 5.

2. Quoted in Fitzroy Maclean, *Scotland: A Concise History*. London, England: Thames and Hudson Ltd., 1993, p. 10.

3. Quoted in Maclean, *Scotland*, p. 22.

CHAPTER 3: THE MONARCHY

4. Quoted in Maclean, *Scotland*, p. 27.

5. Quoted in Meek, *The Land and People of Scotland*, p. 114.

6. Quoted in Meek, *The Land and People of Scotland*, p. 118.

7. Quoted in Maclean, *Scotland*, p. 56.

CHAPTER 4: UNION AND THEREAFTER

8. Quoted in Maclean, *Scotland*, p. 134.

9. Quoted in Maclean, *Scotland*, p. 156.

10. Quoted in Maclean, *Scotland*, p. 171.

11. Quoted in Meek, *The Land and People of Scotland*, p. 160.

12. Quoted in Maclean, *Scotland*, p. 200.

CHAPTER 5: SCOTLAND TODAY

13. Meek, *The Land and People of Scotland*, p. 1.

14. Peter L. Payne, "The Economy," in *Scotland in the 20th Century*, eds. T. M. Devine and R. J. Finlay. Edinburgh, Scotland: Edinburgh University Press, 1997, p. 28.

15. Derek Lambie, "Professor Calls for Drugs to Be Legalised," *The Scottish Express*, October 16, 1998. www.ukcia.org.

16. Graham Walker, "Varieties of Scottish Protestant Identities," in Devine and Finlay, *Scotland in the 20th Century*, p. 251.

CHAPTER 6: POPULAR CULTURE

17. Robert Burns, "Address to a Haggis," *The Bard: The Complete Guide to the Immortal Memory of Scotland's Greatest Poet.* www.rabbie-burns.com.

18. Burns, "Address to a Haggis."

19. Darwin Porter and Danforth Prince, *Frommer's Scotland,* 4th ed. New York: Macmillan, 1998, p. 33.

EPILOGUE: REBIRTH OF A NATION

20. Quoted in Associated Press, "Queen Opens Scottish Parliament," *New York Times,* July 1, 1999. www.nyt.com.

21. Quoted in Murray Ritchie, "The Rebirth of a Nation," *The Herald* (Edinburgh), July 2, 1999. www.theherald.co.uk.

22. Peter Hennessy, "Revival Through Revolution," *Time,* May 10, 1999. http://cgi.pathfinder.com/time/magazine.

23. Quoted in "Today Is a Proud Moment: A New Stage of a Journey Begun Long Ago," *The Times* (London), July 2, 1999. www.the-times.co.uk.

24. Quoted in Scottish National Party Archive, "Ewen Begins Conference Buildup With Poster Launch," September 16, 1996. www.snp.org.uk.

25. Robert Louis Stevenson, *The Silverado Squatters.* London: Chattus and Windus, 1884. Full text available from http://sunsite.berkeley.edu.

CHRONOLOGY

B.C.

ca. 7000
Mesolithic (Middle Stone Age) people begin to settle in Scotland.

ca. 4500
Neolithic (New Stone Age) people arrive and begin to form agricultural communities.

ca. 1800
Bronze Age people start using improved metalworking techniques.

ca. 300
Celts begin settling in Scotland.

A.D.

81
Agricola leads Roman troops on first invasion of Scotland.

84
Romans withdraw from Central Lowland region.

121
Romans begin building Hadrian's Wall to serve as protection against invaders from Scotland.

397
Saint Ninian establishes first Christian monastery at Whithorn.

ca. 450
Anglo-Saxon tribes begin invading British Isles.

500
Scots, having immigrated from Ireland, consolidate power in the southwest.

ca. 550
Angles settle in Southern Uplands, ousting the Britons.

563
Saint Columba establishes abbey on island of Iona.

789
Vikings begin raids on Scotland; they eventually establish
settlements in the far north and in the Western Isles.

843
Kenneth McAlpin unites the thrones of Scots and Picts.

1018
Malcolm II conquers Angles and absorbs Lothian into
kingdom of Scotland.

1034
Duncan adds Strathclyde to the kingdom.

1071
William I of England invades Scotland.

1124–53
David I imposes English feudal system on southern Scotland.

1165
William I "the Lion" enters into what will become the "Auld
Alliance" with France.

1174
William the Lion is forced to sign the Treaty of Falaise making Scotland subject to England.

1189
Richard I "the Lionheart" of England restores Scottish independence.

1266
Norway cedes Western Isles to Scotland.

1290
Edward I of England places John Balliol on the Scottish
throne.

1295
Edward I defeats Balliol at Dunbar and takes the Stone of
Scone to England.

1297
William Wallace leads Scottish rebellion against English.

1306
Robert I "the Bruce" is crowned king.

1314
Robert I defeats Edward II of England at Bannockburn.

1320
Scots proclaim their independence in the Declaration of Abroath.

1326
First Scottish Parliament meets.

1328
England recognizes Scottish independence in the Treaty of Northampton.

1371
Robert II, first of the Stewart line, is crowned king.

1411
Saint Andrew's University is founded.

1432
Orkney and Shetland Islands become part of Scotland.

1488
James IV becomes king; he introduces the Renaissance into Scotland.

1502
James IV marries Margaret Tudor of England.

1513
English defeat Scots at the Battle of Flodden; James IV is killed.

1542
James V dies after defeat of Scots at Solway Moss, leaving throne to infant Mary Queen of Scots.

1557
Lords of the Congregation sign First Covenant to establish a national Protestant Church.

1560
Mary returns from France to rule; Parliament establishes the Church of Scotland.

1567
Mary is forced to renounce Scottish throne in favor of her infant son, James VI.

1603
James VI of Scotland also becomes King James I of England.

1638
Hundreds of Scots sign National Covenant to maintain the Presbyterian Church.

1651
Oliver Cromwell's troops defeat the Scottish army of Charles II at Worcester.

1691
William III forces Scottish lords to sign an oath of allegiance.

1692
Campbell troops massacre MacDonald clansmen at Glencoe.

1707
Act of Union merges England and Scotland into United Kingdom.

1715
Jacobites rebel and are defeated at Battle of Sheriffmuir.

1746
Duke of Cumberland defeats Jacobite forces of "Bonnie Prince Charlie" at Battle of Culloden.

1769
James Watt patents steam engine.

1776
Adam Smith writes *An Inquiry into the Nature and Causes of the Wealth of Nations.*

1786
Robert Burns publishes *Poems, Chiefly in the Scots Dialect.*

1802
World's first practical steamship is launched in Scotland.

1814
Sir Walter Scott publishes his first novel, *Waverley.*

1888
James Kier Hardie founds the Scottish Labour Party.

1934
Scottish National Party is founded.

1969
Oil discovered under floor of the North Sea.

1997
Scots vote to restore separate Parliament.

1999
Queen Elizabeth II opens Scottish Parliament on July 1.

Suggestions for Further Reading

Books

Elwood D. Baumann, *The Loch Ness Monster*. New York: Franklin Watts, 1972. A discussion of the sightings of and the searches for the fabled monster supposedly dwelling in the Scottish loch.

Susan Cooper, *The Boggart*. New York: M. K. McElderry Books, 1993. A Canadian girl visits a castle her family inherited in Scotland and encounters the boggart, a mischievous spirit.

———, *The Boggart and the Monster*. New York: M. K. McElderry Books, 1997. Sequel to *The Boggart* in which the Scottish spirit seeks to save his cousin, the Loch Ness Monster.

Mollie Hunter, *The King's Swift Rider: A Novel on Robert the Bruce*. New York: HarperCollins Juvenile Books, 1998. A fanciful tale about a young boy who saves the life of King Robert I and then accompanies him on his adventures.

George MacDonald, *Alec Forbes and His Friend Annie*. Edited by Michael Phillips. Minneapolis, MN: Bethany House Publishers, 1990. An adaptation of a story by a nineteenth-century Scottish storyteller that describes the adventures of an orphaned girl and her unusual friend.

Robert Louis Stevenson, *Kidnapped*. New York: Charles Scribner's Sons, 1982. Later printing of the 1913 edition featuring illustrations by N. C. Wyeth. This classic novel relates the exciting adventures of young David Balfour's journey across Scotland to regain his rightful inheritance.

WORKS CONSULTED

H. D. Black, *A Geography of Scotland.* London, England: Cambridge University Press, 1984. A highly technical examination of settlement and land use with an abundance of photographs and charts.

Alan Bold, *Scottish Tartans.* Andover, England: Pitkin Guides, 1997. A brief examination of the history of Highland dress. This book includes descriptions of many of the more popular clan tartans.

John Burnett, *Sporting Scotland.* Edinburgh, Scotland: National Museums of Scotland, 1995. A small but fact-filled book on the history of sports in Scotland. Surprisingly little attention is paid to golf.

Roderick D. Cannon, *The Highland Bagpipe and Its Music.* Edinburgh, Scotland: John Donald Publishers Ltd., 1995. A thorough examination of the history of bagpipes and bagpipe music.

T. M. Devine and R. J. Finlay, eds., *Scotland in the 20th Century.* Edinburgh, Scotland: Edinburgh University Press, 1997. A scholarly examination of the various facets of modern Scottish life. Each chapter in this informative book is written by an expert in the field.

Richard Killeen, *A Short History of Scotland.* Dublin, Ireland: Gill & Macmillan Ltd., 1994. A concise and well-illustrated history of Scotland that presents a large amount of data in a small volume.

W. Kinnear and G. C. Wright, *Our Scotland.* London, England: Thomas Nelson and Sons Ltd., 1969. This thorough study of the geography of Scotland includes region-by-region descriptions of agriculture and industry.

K. J. Lea, *A Geography of Scotland.* North Pomfret, VT: David & Charles, 1977. An excellent source for topographical and climatic data of Scotland.

105

J. D. Mackie, *A History of Scotland.* New York: Dorset Press, 1978. The revised and updated edition of a work originally published in 1964. One of the most authoritative works on Scotland.

Fitzroy Maclean, *Scotland: A Concise History.* London, England: Thames and Hudson Ltd., 1993. An excellent, comprehensive, and well-illustrated history of Scotland from prehistoric times to the twentieth century.

Magnus Magnusson and Graham White, eds., *The Nature of Scotland.* Edinburgh, Scotland: Canongate Books, 1991. This description of the land, plants, and animals of Scotland is lavishly illustrated with color photographs.

Seumas Macneill and Thomas Pearston, *Tutor for the Highland Bagpipe.* West Calder, Scotland: Hugh K. Clarkson & Sons Ltd., 1997. This publication of Scotland's College of Piping goes into great detail on the construction and playing of bagpipes.

James McCarthy, *Wild Scotland.* Edinburgh, Scotland: Luath Press Ltd., 1995. Contains a very detailed description of the animals and plants found in Scotland with dozens of color photographs.

James Meek, *The Land and People of Scotland,* Portraits of the Nations series. New York: J. B. Lippincott, 1990. Extremely well-written and comprehensive overview of Scottish life, culture, and history.

Darwin Porter and Danforth Prince, *Frommer's Scotland,* 4th ed. New York: Macmillan, 1998. This guidebook is intended for the traveler and deals mostly with sites, restaurants, and hotels, but it also has informative sections on history and culture.

Rosalyn Thiro, ed., *Scotland.* London, England: Dorling Kindersley Limited, 1999. A comprehensive and highly entertaining travel guide with introductory sections on sports, food, history, geology, and many other aspects of Scottish life.

Periodicals and Internet Sources

Associated Press, "Queen Opens Scottish Parliament," *New York Times,* July 1, 1999. www.nyt.com.

Robert Burns, "Address to a Haggis," *The Bard: The Complete Guide to the Immortal Memory of Scotland's Most Famous Poet.* www.rabbie-burns.com.

Gillian Harris, "Kilted Connery Cocks a Snook at Dress Code," *The Times* (London), July 2, 1999.

Peter Hennessy, "Revival Through Revolution," *Time*, May 10, 1999. http://cgi.pathfinder.com/time/magazine.

Derek Lambie, "Professor Calls for Drugs to Be Legalised," *The Scottish Express*, October 16, 1998, U.K. Cannabis Internet Activists. www.ukcia.org.

Murray Ritchie, "The Rebirth of a Nation," *The Herald* (Edinburgh), July 2, 1999. www.theherald.co.uk.

Scottish National Party Archive, "Ewen Begins Conference Buildup with Poster Launch," September 16, 1996. www.snp.org.uk.

Robert Louis Stevenson, *The Silverado Squatters.* London, England: Chaltus and Windus, 1884. Full text available from http://sunsite.berkeley.edu.

(No author), "Today Is a Proud Moment: A New Stage of a Journey Begun Long Ago," *The Times* (London), July 2, 1999. www.the-times.co.uk.

INDEX

PICTURE CREDITS

ABOUT THE AUTHOR

William W. Lace is a native of Fort Worth, Texas. He holds a bachelor's degree from Texas Christian University, a master's from East Texas State University, and a doctorate from the University of North Texas. After working for newspapers in Baytown, Texas, and Fort Worth, he joined the University of Texas at Arlington as sports information director and later became the director of the news service. He is now executive assistant to the chancellor for the Tarrant County College District in Fort Worth. He and his wife, Laura, live in Arlington and have two children. Lace has written numerous other works for Lucent Books, one of which—*The Death Camps* in the Holocaust Library series—was selected by the New York Public Library for its 1999 Recommended Teenage Reading List.